MEDITERRANEAN
FLAVORS

MEDITERRANEAN FLAVORS

Recipes from the Countries of the Sun

Maria José Sevilla

Illustrated by
Christopher Wormell

Clarkson Potter/Publishers
New York

For my mother

Published by Clarkson N. Potter, Inc., 201 East 50th Street, New York,
New York 10022. Member of the Crown Publishing Group.

Random House, Inc., New York, Toronto, London, Sydney, Auckland
Originally published in 1995 in England by Pavilion Books, Ltd.
26 Upper Ground, London, England

Clarkson N. Potter, Potter, and colophon are trademarks of
Clarkson N. Potter, Inc.

Manufactured in Singapore
Conceived and designed by
The Artworks Press Limited

Library of Congress Cataloging-in-Publication Data
is available upon request.

ISBN 0-517-70203-7
10 9 8 7 6 5 4 3 2 1
First American Edition

CONTENTS

INTRODUCTION

Until 1975 the foods of the western end of the Mare Nostrum – Catalonia, Andalusia, the Spanish Levant, Languedoc, Provence and the northern tip of Morocco – made up my Mediterranean universe. Then I visited the eastern Aegean: what a treat was in store for me. This book is the result of the many consequent to-ings and fro-ings across the Mediterranean Sea. My encounters with these places, linked by history, climate and water, have enabled me to recognize common culinary themes as well as interesting variations from one culture to the next. Once I understood the relevance of the ingredients and the cooking methods that define the flavours of Mediterranean food then I began to imagine a map which would reveal the food secrets of this culture. It would be a map without political boundaries; its language one of quince, oregano, black pepper, cumin seeds, garlic and wine. It would have little to do with the capricious physical boundaries that have been drawn up, often arbitrarily, down the centuries. Instead, its natural borders would be defined by culture, ingredients and tradition.

These ideas came together for me when I first saw an aubergine (eggplant) of the most extravagant purple in a linocut by Christopher Wormell. I began imagining the shapes and colours of the key foods in Mediterranean cuisine: those which I associate with the flavours of the sun. Soon these essential, characteristic ingredients became the titles of chapters: a fruit or vegetable, olive oil, wine or fish, a pomegranate, a garlic clove, a flat bread or a pine nut. In turn each chapter would include a number of recipes based on the ingredients of the title.

In this book I have expressed, in my own culinary language, everything I have learnt from my wanderings and related that knowledge to my own Spanish culture and to the way I work in the kitchen. Many of the recipes are linked to one another, some come from my family and friends and others are new ways of preparing traditional dishes. I have taken into consideration the flavours of popular and festive food, the flavours of the countryside and of the city, but above all I have given pride of place to the ingredients.

Having now tasted all the recipes in this book I have become very partial to certain preparations which I consider most representative of the Mediterranean cuisine. The essential ingredients have consistently been olive oil, lemon juice, spices, fresh herbs and the exquisitely mellow vinegars of Modena, and the powerful, complex Sherry vinegars of southern Spain. My favourite combinations are preserved lemons in lemon juice and salt (see page 94), olives marinated with bitter orange (see page 22), tuna escabeche (see page 32), pickled anchovies (see page 42), *harissa* sauce (see page 111) – the list never ends. A number of these are preserved foods: an essential part of the life and lore of Mediterranean people, particularly in the countryside. Cheeses, cured meats and yogurt are also very important. Although in general terms there is less need to preserve food to survive, the economic and political situation varies in the countries of the Mediterranean. To collect in times of plenty and to preserve for the winter months is not a thing of the past. It is promising that many are beginning to treasure artisan- as well as industrially-produced food and are prepared to pay the price for it because it is made with love and with responsibility for the environment.

Although I have developed a healthy appetite for all things Mediterranean, I have to confess a certain weakness for the islands of Majorca and Sicily, the Spanish region of Andalusia, and the countries of Tunisia and Turkey. I sense a special affinity with these places. Maybe it is

due to shared history, the way people smile or because I cannot resist the sweets and pastries of a particular village. I constantly look forward to discovering new areas and new faces.

A NOTE ON UTENSILS

To me traditional utensils, and earthenware pots in particular, are utterly irresistible. I always cook with them, as my mother still does, and consequently I'm always breaking them! Earthenware utensils are used for cooking and serving all over the Mediterranean world. Very often the pot lends its name to a dish. In Spain a *cazuela de pescado* is both the pot and a fish stew. In North Africa a *tagine* is a shallow casserole of earthenware or metal, and is also the name given to the many different meals cooked in this dish. In Morocco vegetable, meat and fish stews are cooked in a glazed earthenware shallow dish with a marvellous conical top called a *tagine slaouis*. In Greece the *yiouvetsi* is the traditional earthenware pot in which pasta and meat dishes are baked in the oven. Similarly, there is the *pagen* of fish in Egypt, the *tian* of vegetables in southern France and the *greixonera* of fish in Majorca. I normally use a boring but efficient metal *couscousière* because I am frightened to break the unique green pot I bought in the Medina in Tunis but I can assure you that food tastes better in the traditional Mediterranean pots.

GARLIC, HERBS AND SPICES

Garlic, a highly aromatic member of the lily family, originated in the east, in the region of Kirgiz in Central Asia, and travelled to the Middle East, Egypt and the lands under Greek and Roman domination. The ancient Greeks referred to it as the 'stinking rose'. What a perfect illustration of the love and hate garlic arouses in people. Other descriptions such as the 'truffle' or the 'camphor of the poor' have also been used in the past. As far as I am concerned, my cooking would be lost without garlic, particularly the rosy variety which is the one I prefer.

With my romantic and slightly liberal approach to food history, I like to believe that garlic made its appearance in Mediterranean cuisine one day somewhere to the north-west of that beloved sea. The players in this scenario were a mortar and pestle, a man or woman, some cloves of garlic and olive oil. The resulting recipe is now prepared all over the Mediterranean under many different names, of which I prefer *all-i-oli*. This time-honoured sauce delights and improves fish, meat and vegetable dishes made with ingredients from the colourful markets of Catalonia, Italy and the South of France. In other places, with African or Turkish influences, garlic is used with less enthusiasm.

All-i-oli in Catalan or *ajiaceite* in Castilian (*ajo* means garlic in the Castilian language) refers to a perfect, but difficult to achieve, emulsion of pounded garlic, salt and olive oil (see page 114). This paste is served with barbecued meat – particularly rabbit, rice dishes and fish and shellfish stews. In France, egg yolks are added and this is called *aïoli*; it is eaten with vegetables, egg dishes, fish stews and, above all, lobster. The people from the Balearic Islands go even further by making a clear distinction between an emulsion made with garlic and olive oil, and one of garlic, olive oil and egg yolk. The first is *all-i-oli* and the second is *all-i-oli amb ou*. Perfectly clear! We can even confuse the issue a little more by making an *all-i-oli* called *negat*. In this case the desired result is a diluted sauce – not a perfect emulsion at all.

Garlic and olive oil sauces are used in different ways around the Mediterranean depending on the regional specialities. In Spain small bowls of *all-i-oli* are served with shellfish or rice dishes, such as *arroz negro* (black rice) or the Alicantine *abanda* rice. One or two spoonfuls of the sauce can be added to a dish just before it leaves the kitchen; this is how the French serve the tasty vegetable combinations called *aïoli*, and *bourride*, a superb white fish soup from Provence. Or it can be added while cooking to bring out the flavours of traditional fish and potato stews (see page 126) such as the Catalan *semi-tomba* or the *bacalao a la Catalana*. In the latter, *allioli negat* is added 4 or 5 minutes before the dish is ready.

Leaving the western shores and travelling to the land of the Ligurians, a recipe from the port of Genoa brings new flavours to the basic olive oil and garlic sauce. *Pesto alla Genovese* is an irresistible combination of basil, pine kernels, Parmesan cheese, olive oil and garlic (see page 20). If fresh basil is available, this easy-to-prepare yet unique combination will make you a pasta wizard.

Caçik brings back memories of the Turkish peninsula of Daça, a delightful place where the food is simply superb. This is a refreshing cucumber (hothouse English cucumber) salad with a yogurt, garlic and dill sauce, garnished with olive oil and dried mint. A similar dish is the Greek *tzatziki* (see page 25). The crucial difference between these two dishes is that in *caçik* the olive oil is used as a dressing while in *tzatziki* it is mixed in with the garlic and vinegar.

New sauces were created with the arrival of tomatoes and peppers from the Americas in the sixteenth century. *Rouille* (see page 144) is a hot reddish sauce that ably accompanies fish and shellfish stews, particularly *bouillabaisse.* To prepare *rouille,* chili pepper and sweet green pepper are simmered in water until tender, drained and then blended with roasted sweet red peppers, garlic, olive oil and breadcrumbs. A little of the sauce is placed on top of the dish before serving.

Garlic and hot chili peppers preserved in olive oil and served with couscous take us south to the African coast and the lands of the fiery *harissa* (see page 111). Many years ago as a student I tasted this powerful sauce in a modest Moroccan restaurant outside Toulouse. Today a jug of the most delicious *harissa,* bought recently in Tunis, is treated with respect by my family who often search the fridge looking for something exciting to eat. And I do not need to go to Rome to become a true follower of the *aio e oio,* the traditional olive oil, garlic and chili pepper sauce served with pasta.

While peppers had an easy time, adopted and adapted by the cooks of the Old World, the tomato was regarded with suspicion for centuries. Historians are still arguing about the moment when tomatoes and garlic were successfully combined in a sauce better known as *pizzaiola. Pizzaoiola* is another way of covering a piece of bread with something very tasty: an old and healthy Mediterranean custom. In this case (see page 68) the bread dough is baked together with the *pizzaiola*.

There are many other combinations in which garlic is the common ingredient, all equally delicious and all traditional. Sometimes they follow medieval recipes to the letter, sometimes they are prepared with a modern approach. A few months ago I read a delightful essay on garlic soup. As a Spaniard I had always thought that this humble water, olive oil, bread and little-else soup was prescribed only out of necessity in my country. I was surprised to find that the recipe created to utilize stale, left-over bread was popular all around the Mediterranean Sea (see page 26).

Ajo blanco (see page 18) is a great legacy of the seventh-century Moorish occupation of the Iberian Peninsula. This dish is a cold gazpacho of bread, garlic, olive oil, vinegar, water and almonds. It appears that *ajo blanco* is a first cousin of the beloved *shorothalmi* of the ancient Athenians, known as *skorthalia* today. *Skorthalia* is a sauce and not a soup which uses walnuts instead of almonds.

Recipes calling for dozens of garlic cloves can take us from village to village, but generally chicken-based dishes are found north of the Pyrenees in the lands of the *poulet aux quarente gousses d'ail*. If lamb is preferred, we will have to cross the mountains and head south into the land of the Catalans and the Aragons. Delicious tasting time could be spent going back and forth across mountains, valleys and the Mediterranean Sea looking for garlic recipes. For example, *ajoarriero*, a second cousin of the *brandade*, combines another set of classic Mediterranean flavours: garlic, olive oil and salted cod . . . I could go on and on.

FOR THE BEST RESULTS WHEN USING GARLIC,

FOLLOW THESE SIMPLE TIPS:

Look for young garlic in the spring; violet varieties are the best.
Remove the green parts inside when the garlic is old.
If you prefer a gentle aroma use whole garlic cloves.
You can also blanch the peeled cloves and use them
as if they were fresh.
Try to avoid using a garlic press.
Burnt garlic is to be avoided.

WHITE ALMOND SOUP WITH PRAWNS / SHRIMP, MUSHROOMS AND FRESH HERBS

This almond soup is a departure from the succulent cold soup, known as ajo blanco, prepared in the Andalusian provinces of Málaga and Córdoba. Here the taste of garlic is lighter and less aggressive. I first tasted this very modern approach to a traditional dish at the Restaurant El Bulli in Catalonia.

SERVES 2

11 RAW KING OR TIGER PRAWNS (LARGE SHRIMP) IN SHELL

100 ML / 3½ FL OZ / 7 TABLESPOONS WATER

1 GARLIC CLOVE, PEELED

80 G / 2½ OZ / ½ CUP FRESH (RAW) ALMONDS, PEELED

SALT AND FRESHLY GROUND PEPPER

750 ML / 1¼ PINTS / 3 CUPS OLIVE OIL, PLUS EXTRA FOR SAUTÉING

A FEW DROPS OF SHERRY VINEGAR

1 TABLESPOON FRESH PARSLEY, CHOPPED

2 MEDIUM-SIZED FRESH CEPS (BOLETUS EDULIS / PORCINI) OR ANOTHER TYPE OF MUSHROOM, CLEANED AND THINLY SLICED

FOR THE ALMOND AND ASPARAGUS SALAD:

8 ASPARAGUS TIPS

½ TABLESPOON SHERRY VINEGAR

2 TABLESPOONS OLIVE OIL

15 FRESH (RAW) ALMONDS, PEELED

1 TABLESPOON FRESH MINT, CHOPPED

A PINCH OF FRESH DILL

Boil 5 of the king prawns in the water for a few minutes; do not overcook. Strain and set the stock aside. (Use the prawns in another recipe.)

To prepare the white almond soup, use an electric blender. First blanch the garlic in boiling water for 2 minutes. Work the almonds, blanched garlic, prawn stock and a pinch of salt in the blender. When smooth, begin adding the olive oil little by little, without stopping the blender. Add the Sherry vinegar and the parsley. Set aside.

Peel and de-vein the remaining raw king prawns. Blanch the asparagus for 2 to 3 minutes, then refresh under cool running water and drain.

Season the mushrooms with salt and pepper. Heat a dash of olive oil in a small frying pan and sauté the mushrooms on both sides for a few seconds. Using another pan, sauté the king prawns in a little oil.

Mix the Sherry vinegar with a dash of olive oil and pour over the almonds and asparagus, tossing in the mint and dill. Place the almond, asparagus and herb salad in soup plates. Pour in the white almond soup and carefully place the king prawns and mushrooms on top. Add a little more olive oil and serve.

BASIL, GARLIC AND PARMESAN CHEESE SAUCE

If you do not have a mortar and pestle, stop reading and go and buy yourself one! Once you have used it, you will find it is a friend for life – especially when you try this exquisite pesto sauce with your favourite pasta.

MAKES ABOUT 350 ML / 12 FL OZ / 1½ CUPS

150 G / 5 OZ / ABOUT ⅔ CUP FRESH ITALIAN BASIL LEAVES, ROUGHLY CHOPPED

3 GARLIC CLOVES, PEELED AND CHOPPED

2 TABLESPOONS PINE NUTS

60 G / 2 OZ / ½ CUP FRESHLY GRATED PARMESAN CHEESE

SALT AND FRESHLY GROUND BLACK PEPPER

300 ML / 10 FL OZ / 1¼ CUPS OLIVE OIL

Pound the basil, garlic and pine nuts until you have a smooth paste. Add the Parmesan cheese, salt and pepper and pound a little more. Add the oil, drop by drop, as you would for *allioli*. Stored in an airtight container in the refrigerator, the sauce will keep for up to 10 days.

This tends to be a very powerful, flavoursome, thick paste, so mix in a little water before you add the sauce to the pasta.

ROASTED CEPS AND GARLIC HEADS

If you are an adventurous eater and you like mushrooms and garlic, then this is the recipe for you. Ceps (botanical name Boletus edulis) *are also known as porcini.*

SERVES 6 AS A FIRST COURSE

6 SMALL HEADS OF GARLIC

6 BOLETUS EDULIS (CEPS / PORCINI), THE SAME SIZE AS THE GARLIC HEADS, CLEANED AND STALKS TRIMMED A LITTLE

OLIVE OIL

FRESH BREADCRUMBS

1 GARLIC CLOVE, PEELED AND CHOPPED

FRESH PARSLEY, CHOPPED

SALT AND FRESHLY GROUND BLACK PEPPER

Cut the garlic heads across in half; discard the top halves or keep them for another recipe. Cut a thin slice off the base of each bottom half, to make it flat. Then remove the core and a few small cloves from the centre to make a little hollow. Set a mushroom on top of each garlic half, inserting the stalk into the hollow. Arrange on a baking tray. Drizzle with a little olive oil and place the baking tray in the oven preheated to 150°C / 300°F / gas mark 2. Roast for about 10 minutes.

Mix some breadcrumbs with a little chopped garlic and parsley and season with salt and pepper. Remove the baking tray from the oven and place a little of the parsley mixture on top of each mushroom. Add a little more olive oil and roast for another 10 minutes. Transfer the garlic to a serving dish.

Whisk the juices and oil left in the tray and pour on top of each mushroom. Serve very hot.

MARINATED OLIVES

In southern Spain, fresh olives are prepared this way during the olive harvest. Fresh olives are available at the beginning of autumn in many shops; however, quality olives that have already been prepared can also be used and won't need to be soaked.

3–4 KG / 6–8 LB FRESH OLIVES, SLIGHTLY CRUSHED

1 BITTER ORANGE OR SEVILLE ORANGE, CUT INTO PIECES WITH PEEL INTACT, ANY SEEDS DISCARDED (SWEET ORANGE CAN BE USED IF BITTER ORANGES OR SEVILLE ORANGES ARE NOT AVAILABLE)

½ DRIED RED SWEET PEPPER, SUCH AS CHORICEROS OR ANCHO, SOAKED IN WATER FOR 2 HOURS AND SEEDS REMOVED

1 HEAD OF GARLIC, 2 CLOVES PEELED AND THE REST PEELED AND CRUSHED

2 TEASPOONS CUMIN SEEDS

2 PICKLED CUCUMBERS, CHOPPED

2 CARROTS

½ TEASPOON DRIED OREGANO

1 GREEN SWEET PEPPER, SEEDED AND CHOPPED

2–3 LEAVES FROM A FENNEL BULB, CHOPPED

A LITTLE WINE VINEGAR

Soak the olives for 8 days, changing the water several times.

Pound in a mortar and pestle the orange, soaked and dried red pepper, 2 peeled garlic cloves and cumin seeds to make a coarse paste. Cook the carrots in boiling water with garlic, a little lemon, thyme, salt and a small hot chili pepper, and then chop. Add the pounded ingredients to the pickled cucumbers and carrots together with the crushed

garlic, oregano, pieces of green pepper and the fennel. Add the wine vinegar.

Place the olives in a large bowl and season with a little salt. Add the marinade. Pour in a little fresh water if necessary, to ensure that the olives are totally immersed in liquid. Leave to marinate for 3 days.

GRILLED AUBERGINES / EGGPLANTS WITH A FRESH MINT AND BALSAMIC VINEGAR DRESSING

You can prepare this dish with baby aubergines (eggplants) which are often available in local markets and ethnic shops. These don't have to be peeled or salted.

SERVES 4 AS A FIRST COURSE

2 YOUNG AUBERGINES (EGGPLANTS)

SALT

6 TABLESPOONS EXTRA-VIRGIN OLIVE OIL

1 TABLESPOON BALSAMIC VINEGAR

5–6 FRESH MINT LEAVES, CHOPPED

2 GARLIC CLOVES, PEELED, BLANCHED AND CHOPPED

Cut the aubergines across into 1 cm / ½ inch slices. Place them in a colander, sprinkle with 2 teaspoons salt and leave to drain for about 30 minutes. Rinse the aubergines and pat dry with paper towels. Brush them with a little of the olive oil, place under a preheated grill (broiler) and cook for 5 to 6 minutes on each side or until charred and tender.

Meanwhile, mix together the rest of the oil, the vinegar, mint, garlic and a little salt.

Dress the aubergines, while hot, with this mixture, then set aside to cool. Serve with roasted sweet peppers and onions and a yogurt and cucumber dip.

YOGURT AND CUCUMBER DIP

SERVES 4 TO 6

200 G / 7 OZ GREEK STRAINED YOGURT (1 CUP VERY THICK PLAIN YOGURT)

2 TABLESPOONS WATER

1 GARLIC CLOVE, PEELED AND CRUSHED

SALT

125 G / 4 OZ CUCUMBERS (HOTHOUSE ENGLISH CUCUMBERS), PEELED AND FINELY CHOPPED

DRIED OR FRESHLY CHOPPED MINT

½ TABLESPOON OLIVE OIL

Whisk the yogurt to a smooth cream, adding the water little by little to achieve a light consistency, on the soupy side. Add the garlic and season with salt. Add the cucumber and mix thoroughly.

Serve chilled, garnished with a pinch of mint and drops of olive oil.

A DIFFERENT GARLIC SOUP

I wondered if I should call this recipe a soup or a meal with two courses.
If you have time on your hands bake some Inca biscuits (see page 70) and use
them instead of the slices of fresh bread.

SERVES 8

1 ONION, PEELED AND CHOPPED

3 LEEKS, CHOPPED

4 TABLESPOONS OLIVE OIL, PLUS EXTRA FOR DRIZZLING

2 TOMATOES, PEELED, SEEDED AND CRUSHED

4 GARLIC CLOVES, PEELED AND CRUSHED

2 SPRIGS OF FRESH HERB FENNEL, CHOPPED

1 TEASPOON DICED ORANGE PEEL

A BUNCH OF MIXED FRESH HERBS (EG. PARSLEY, THYME, MARJORAM, CHIVES), CHOPPED

4 POTATOES, PEELED AND ROUGHLY CHOPPED

8 SAFFRON THREADS, SOAKED IN A LITTLE BOILED WATER FOR 20 MINUTES

2.4 LITRES / 4 PINTS / 2½ QUARTS WATER

SALT AND FRESHLY GROUND BLACK PEPPER

8 EGGS

4 SLICES OF FRESH BREAD

Fry the onion and leeks in a little olive oil for 10 to 15 minutes or until slightly coloured. Add the tomatoes, garlic, fennel, orange peel, mixed herbs, potatoes and saffron. Pour in the water, season generously with salt and pepper, and bring to the boil. Simmer until the potatoes are tender, then remove them from the broth. (Do not worry if some of the potatoes remain in the soup or if some of the vegetables end up in the potatoes.) Mash the potatoes and add the chopped parsley. Poach the eggs (one per person) in the broth.

Chop the bread into small pieces or sops, and put about half a slice in each bowl. Ladle the soup into the bowls on top of the bread. Serve the mashed potatoes separately, each serving topped with a poached egg and drizzled with a little extra-virgin olive oil.

OLIVE OIL, VINEGARS AND MARINADES

To me the olive signifies winter: cold, aggressive but dry weather, incredible light, vast sweeps of rolling hills covered with old trees and morning dew, small white buildings or black Berber tents in the distance. Sometimes the trees are scattered and free and at other times they are aligned like soldiers of a silent and immobile army. Winter also means fried or grilled fish, roasted sweet peppers, bread with olive oil and sugar, sweet oranges dressed simply with the best olive oil of the harvest, and olives marinated in many different ways (see page 22).

Wild olive trees were always present around the Mediterranean lands. The Phoenicians and Greeks brought the first grafting techniques to the western shores, the Phoenicians sailing via Africa and the Greeks along the European coast. Later the cultivation of the olive and production of olive oil became an agricultural policy of the Roman Empire. But that was a long time ago . . . Today the importance of olive oil as a healthy and tasty ingredient has been recognized all over the world. For once, trading demands and new technology have offered a friendly hand to its production. The result is quality oils of great diversity and character which bring excitement to the kitchen and enjoyment to the table. When I talk about olive oil I mean extra-virgin olive oil. I use it for frying, stewing, sautéing, making dressings, sauces and marinades and also for baking bread.

Olive oil has always been the main source of fat in Greece, the South of France, Spain and Italy. In Morocco it is used primarily in cold dishes and salads and in the preparation of *harissa* (see page 111). Olive oil is also an important feature in Turkish food. Other types of vegetable oil, pork fat, butter, clarified butter and *alya*, the rendered fat from the tails of sheep, are used to a lesser degree in Mediterranean recipes.

Preserving food for the winter or for just a few days, dressing vegetables and salads and marinading fish, meats and all kinds of vegetables are part of our cookery inheritance. In the Mediterranean, preserving food is an art loved by all: vinegar, olive oil, salt and brine have been used to flavour and keep food since time immemorial. The lemon came later, both to complement other ingredients and to work as an alternative to vinegar. Garlic, fresh or dried herbs, spices and chilies also play an important part.

I remember Holly Chase, the American specialist on Turkish food, writing with passion and sorrow about the loss of a particular vegetable pickle seller in Istanbul, her memory of his stall is strongly evocative: 'blown glass jars artfully packed with stuffed red peppers, tiny aubergines, beet-dyed turnips, and shredded cabbage layered with whole green tomatoes and carrots rivalled the jewellers' windows of the covered Bazaar.' *Biber tursusu* are the traditional Turkish pickled green peppers, prepared with water, vinegar, salt, garlic cloves and dill, and in Spain, green chili peppers in vinegar are known as *guindillas*. In Sicily, aubergines (eggplants) are preserved with vinegar, olive oil, chili peppers, salt, garlic cloves and dried oregano, and in Greece *htapothi toursi* is tender octopus preserved in vinegar.

Vinegar is also an important ingredient in the preparation of other Mediterranean dishes. *Escabeche* is an ancient Spanish word adopted by the French, which refers to a particular method of cooking mainly of fish, game and vegetables. Fresh tuna *escabeche* (see page 32) is tuna fillet cooked in olive oil and vinegar using a sauce of onions and herbs as a base. Patridges and quails *en escabeche* are equally exciting and if you are travelling in Majorca, look for *alberginies escabetxadas*, another aubergine speciality. The aubergines are first fried in olive oil and then cooked in a marinade of vinegar, white wine, a bay leaf, black pepper, garlic and paprika.

I find it difficult to pin down the term 'marinade', it applies to so many different variations on a theme. We marinate meat to be roasted or barbecued, we marinate fish such as anchovies in vinegar to cure them and then olive oil, garlic and parsley (see page 42) for storage. Olives benefit tremendously from the process – I recommend an Andalusian recipe (see page 22) – and try marinating sweet peppers in their own roasting juices with a dash of Balsamic or Sherry vinegar, their taste is unique.

In southern France, and in particular in the Côte Niçoise, a dish of asparagus, artichokes, broccoli, fennel, onions or leeks might appear on the menu of restaurants, ending with the words *en marinade.* This indicates that a single vegetable is first sautéed in olive oil and then cooked in a marinade of wine, water, spices and fresh herbs. It would normally be served as a cold starter with the marinade poured on top. I have also come across an interesting, though somewhat laborious, recipe for *legumes à la grecque*, in which a selection of vegetables such as onions, courgettes (zucchini), and French beans (thin green beans) are cooked one by one in a broth of chicken stock, white wine, lemon juice and fresh herbs. Once more the marinade will be poured on top and the dish allowed to rest in the refrigerator for a few hours. This is fascinating as wine is not an ingredient usually used in Greek vegetable dishes.

Fresh Tuna Escabeche

I have tasted wonderful examples of game escabèche – quails are particularly good – but escabeche prepared with the small white tuna known as Albacore is a cut above the rest. This is a particularly good old recipe from Fernando Córdoba of the restaurant El Faro in Puerto de Santa María.

Serves 6 as a first course, 4 as a main course

750 g / 1½ lb fresh tuna, in one piece

Salt

300 g / 10 oz onions, peeled and chopped

1 small head of garlic, cloves peeled and sliced

2 bay leaves

2 sprigs of fresh thyme

500 ml / 16 fl oz / 2 cups olive oil

200 ml / 7 fl oz / scant cup Sherry vinegar or white wine vinegar

¾ bottle of dry white wine

Season the tuna with a little salt and set aside for 2 hours. Fry the onions and garlic with the bay leaves and thyme in the olive oil until the onions are tender and translucent. They should not be browned.

Place the tuna in a deep flameproof casserole, add the onion *sofrito* and season with salt according to taste. Pour in the vinegar and wine, and add a little water if necessary, to ensure that the tuna is totally covered. Bring to the boil, then reduce the heat and simmer until the tuna is very tender. Remove from the heat. Leaving the tuna in the liquid, allow to cool and then marinate for at least 24 hours.

To serve, remove the tuna from the stock. Slice and dress with a little of the stock. Serve with caramelized yellow peppers and a salad of leaves and roasted vegetables.

CARAMELIZED YELLOW SWEET PEPPERS

*This is a treat. Every Saturday I buy one or two kilos of yellow
peppers in Portobello, which is my local market in London.
I have to confess that I cook these peppers several times a week!*

SERVES 4

OLIVE OIL

4 YELLOW SWEET PEPPERS, CUT IN HALF AND SEEDED

2–3 GARLIC CLOVES, PEELED AND THICKLY SLICED

1 TEASPOON SHERRY VINEGAR

1 TEASPOON PARSLEY, CHOPPED

SALT AND FRESHLY GROUND PEPPER

Heat a film of olive oil in a deep pan. Add the peppers, placing the halves side by side, and brown on both sides. Add the garlic, reduce the heat and cover the pan. Cook over a very low heat for about 30 minutes or until the peppers are tender.

Remove the peppers from the pan and set aside. Deglaze the pan with the Sherry vinegar, and stir in the parsley and seasoning to taste.

Serve the peppers with a drizzling of the Sherry vinegar.

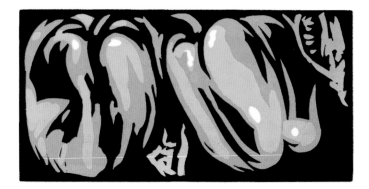

Courgette / Zucchini Flower Fritters

*Only a few kilometres from the city of Barcelona my friend
Carmen Casals collects beautiful courgette flowers early in the
morning, when they are in season. This is the first and most
gratifying part of the day, she says.
This dish is easy to prepare when the flowers are still open.*

SERVES 4 AS AN APPETIZER

8 FLOWERS FROM COURGETTES (ZUCCHINI), OR OTHER SMALL SUMMER SQUASH

250 G / 8 OZ MOZZARELLA DI BUFFALA (BUFFALO MOZZARELLA), CUT INTO 8 SLICES

16 PITTED MARINATED OLIVES (SEE PAGE 22)

FLOUR FOR COATING

1 EGG, BEATEN

BREADCRUMBS FOR COATING

OLIVE OIL FOR FRYING

Fill each flower with slices of mozzarella and a few marinated olives.
Dredge them in flour, dip into egg and coat them with breadcrumbs. Fry
them in about 4 cm / 1½ inches of hot olive oil until golden brown. Drain on
paper towels and serve hot.

STUFFED COURGETTES / ZUCCHINI WITH HAM
AND A PARSLEY SAUCE

The flavour of Spanish Jamón Serrano or the Italian Parma ham
is ideal and traditional in the preparation of vegetable dishes,
but you don't have to use them to enjoy this dish from the rich and varied
repertoire of stuffed vegetables cooked in the Mediterranean.
In Turkey, stuffed vegetables are known as yalanci dolma,
what a promising name!

SERVES 4

8 SMALL COURGETTES (ZUCCHINI)

2 EGGS

100 G / 3½ OZ / ¾ CUP CURED HAM, WITH FAT, FINELY DICED

2 SLICES OF BREAD, SOAKED IN MILK AND SQUEEZED TO REMOVE EXCESS LIQUID

1 GARLIC CLOVE, PEELED AND CHOPPED

30 G / 1 OZ / ½ CUP FRESH PARSLEY, CHOPPED

SALT AND FRESHLY GROUND PEPPER

1 TABLESPOON FRESH CHIVES, CHOPPED

FOR THE PARSLEY SAUCE:

5–6 LARGE PARSLEY STEMS

120 ML / 4 FL OZ / ½ CUP EXTRA-VIRGIN OLIVE OIL

SALT AND FRESHLY GROUND PEPPER

Blanch the courgettes in boiling water for a few minutes. Refresh with cold water and drain. Cut off and discard both tips. Create a tube by carefully removing the central pulp with a very small teaspoon; do not go all the way through – one end should remain covered. Discard the pulp.

In a mixing bowl beat the eggs lightly. Add the ham, soaked bread, garlic and parsley and season with salt and pepper. Mix well. Carefully stuff the courgettes with the mixture. Grease an oven tray and place the courgettes on top. Cover with foil and bake in the oven preheated to 190°C/375°F/gas mark 5 for 30 to 35 minutes.

Meanwhile, to prepare the parsley sauce, put the parsley stems in a bowl and blanch with boiling water two or three times, changing the water each time. Drain well. Blend the parsley stems to a purée, then add the virgin olive oil a little at a time to make a smooth, thick sauce. Season with salt and pepper.

Sprinkle the courgettes with the chopped chives and serve with the parsley sauce.

SALAD OF COD AND WHITE ONIONS
WITH ORANGE-FLAVOURED OIL DRESSING

A good-quality salt cod is essential for making this dish,
the idea for which came from the village of Denia in Valencia.

SERVES 4

300 G / 10 OZ GOOD-QUALITY SALT COD

2 UNWAXED ORANGES

3–4 TABLESPOONS FRUITY EXTRA-VIRGIN OLIVE OIL

3 TABLESPOONS VERY SWEET SHERRY (PEDRO XIMENEZ)

1 TEASPOON BALSAMIC VINEGAR OR SHERRY VINEGAR

1 SMALL WHITE ONION, PEELED AND FINELY SLICED

6–8 FRESH MINT LEAVES

Soak the salt cod in plenty of fresh water for at least 36 hours, changing the water four or five times. Then drain well and remove all skin and bones.

For the orange-flavoured oil, peel one of the oranges thinly (reserve the flesh for the salad), and place the peel in a bowl. Add enough olive oil to cover the peel (3–4 tablespoons). Cover the bowl and set aside to macerate for 24 hours.

To make the dressing, heat the sweet Sherry and boil to reduce by half. Remove from the heat and blend in the balsamic vinegar and 1 tablespoon of the orange-flavoured oil. Leave to cool.

Peel the second orange and either slice or segment both oranges. Arrange on a plate. Slice the cod into thin, almost translucent slices and place them on top of the orange slices. Scatter the sliced onion on top. Dress the salad with the remaining orange-flavoured oil, a few mint leaves and the Sherry dressing. Check the saltiness of the fish before seasoning.

SKATE AND POTATO CAKES WITH A TOMATO VINAIGRETTE

These potato cakes are based on the traditional French and Catalan brandade *which are made with unsalted cod. Here I have used skate.*

SERVES 4 AS A FIRST COURSE

FOR THE CAKES:

4 POTATOES, PEELED AND DICED

1 TABLESPOON OLIVE OIL

1 ONION, PEELED AND SLICED

250 G / 8 OZ POACHED SKATE

4–6 LARGE RED TOMATOES, PEELED, HALVED AND SEEDED

FOR THE VINAIGRETTE:

3 TABLESPOONS EXTRA-VIRGIN OLIVE OIL

1 TABLESPOON CIDER VINEGAR

2 TABLESPOONS FRESH TOMATO PURÉE (PRESS RIPE TOMATOES THROUGH A CHEESE GRATER)

A LITTLE CHOPPED FRESH MINT, PLUS SOME LEAVES TO GARNISH

SALT

Cook the potatoes in boiling salted water until tender; drain and set aside. Heat the olive oil in a frying pan and gently cook the onion until translucent. Stir in the fish and add the potatoes. Using a fork, mash the ingredients until creamy and well amalgamated. Set aside to cool.

Cut the tomato halves into round shapes with a small pastry cutter. Whisk together the ingredients for the vinaigrette.

Shape the cold fish and potato mixture into eight cakes, using your hands, and arrange 4 to 5 tomato shapes on top of each. Drizzle with the fresh tomato vinaigrette, and garnish with fresh mint leaves and serve.

FRESH MINT AND TOMATO SOUP

Wait until summer to prepare this soup, when the tomatoes are ripe and full of flavour. Acidic, pale tomatoes should be avoided.

SERVES *4* TO *6*

4 TABLESPOONS OLIVE OIL

1 GARLIC CLOVE, PEELED AND CHOPPED

1 LARGE GREEN SWEET PEPPER, SEEDED AND CHOPPED

1 KG / 2 LB RIPE TOMATOES, PEELED AND CHOPPED

30 G / 1 OZ CRUSTLESS BROWN BREAD

500 ML / 16 FL OZ / 2 CUPS WATER

1 TABLESPOON FRESH MINT, CHOPPED

SALT

A PINCH OF SUGAR

A FEW DROPS OF BALSAMIC VINEGAR

Heat the olive oil in a large saucepan. Add the garlic and green pepper and fry gently for about 15 minutes or until tender. Add the tomatoes and cook until this *sofrito* is ready (when the tomatoes have cooked down to a pulp). Add the bread to the *sofrito*. Pour in the water, season with salt and add the mint. Bring to the boil, then cover and simmer gently for 25 to 30 minutes.

Blend the soup until smooth. Pass it through a sieve to remove the tomato seeds. Check the seasoning and add a pinch of sugar if the tomatoes are very acidic. Add the vinegar and serve immediately.

MARINATED ANCHOVIES

*Marinated anchovies are a well-known tapa or appetizer,
'Spanish style'. This recipe is different to that used in tapas bars, because
the time taken for the anchovies to be cured in the vinegar has been reduced
from 8 to 2 hours, allowing the taste of the fish to come through.*

SERVES 6 AS A FIRST COURSE

500 G / 1 LB FRESH ANCHOVIES, CLEANED

EXTRA-VIRGIN OLIVE OIL

WHITE WINE VINEGAR

A DASH OF SHERRY VINEGAR

LEMON JUICE

½ GARLIC CLOVE, PEELED AND CHOPPED

1 TABLESPOON FRESH CHIVES, CHOPPED

SALT AND FRESHLY GROUND PEPPER

Remove the bones from the anchovies and fillet them.

Prepare a vinaigrette of two parts olive oil, one part vinegar (plus the Sherry vinegar), a drop of lemon juice, the garlic, chives, salt and pepper. Place the filleted anchovies in a dish and pour over the vinaigrette. Cover and set aside to marinate for about 2 hours.

Serve with a green salad and creamy black olive, anchovy and tuna paste (see page 43).

CREAMY BLACK OLIVE, ANCHOVY AND TUNA PASTE

*A recipe I picked up from my landlady during one summer in the
South of France. Choose good-quality olives which have been
left to ripen on the trees.*

MAKES ABOUT 120 G / 4 OZ / ½ CUP

60 G / 2 OZ GOOD-QUALITY MARINATED PITTED BLACK OLIVES, PACKED IN OLIVE OIL, DRAINED

30 G / 1 OZ CANNED TUNA FISH IN OLIVE OIL, DRAINED

30 G / 1 OZ CANNED ANCHOVIES IN OLIVE OIL, DRAINED

A LITTLE DRIED THYME

A FEW FRESH (RAW) ALMONDS (IF AVAILABLE), SKINNED AND POUNDED

EXTRA-VIRGIN OLIVE OIL TO TASTE

Using an electric blender, make the ingredients into a paste. Use to accompany the marinated anchovies or as a spread on toasted bread.

WINE, THE PERFECT INGREDIENT

My parents would drink wine or spirits only very occasionally at home, but on the shelves beside the stove stood bottles of red and white wine, dry and sweet Sherry, and brandy which very often needed replacing. In the larder were bottles of peaches and pears preserved in red wine, spices and lemon peel and jars of raisins and sultanas (golden raisins) in Sherry. My mother cooked with wine. Following in her footsteps, I too cook fish, meat and game dishes, pasta sauces, desserts and even pastries with this perfect ingredient.

The majority of people believe that, when added to a stew of meat and vegetables, a fish dish or a fruit compote, the condition of the wine is irrelevant. This is not quite so. Wine follows the same principles of quality as any other ingredient. If you are using an inferior or oxidized leftover from the Christmas before last, you can be sure the sauce will be deficient. In addition, beware of so-called cooking wines for they have little to add. Have patience when cooking with wine: wine reduction demands extra care and tasting over the stove but it brings an extra dimension and complexity of flavour to the food.

The vine was cultivated in Mesopotamia from the beginnings of civilization and was brought to Egypt around 3000 BC. In the Greek Empire wine was produced throughout France, Italy, Spain and North Africa. The Romans loved it all. Every single country in the Mediterranean world can make wine but the quality is another matter for agricultural methods, geography and climatic conditions differ considerably from country to country.

Religion has undoubtedly affected the development of viticulture and wine consumption. The Koran forbids alcohol and in the Jewish faith, wine is reserved for ritual. Today it is made in small quantities in Lebanon, Israel, Jordan, Turkey, Egypt, Tunisia and Morocco, but broadly speaking the wine from these countries does not play a part in local culinary traditions. On the other hand in Spain, France, Italy, Cyprus and Greece wine is both a drink and an important cooking ingredient in recipes for soups, rice, pasta sauces, fish and fish stocks, meat and even desserts. As far as vegetables are concerned, there are very few traditional recipes featuring wine although it can increasingly be found in the food prepared in restaurants.

Zuppa di pesce, bouillabaisse, the Catalan fish stew *zarzuela, soupe aux moules* and a great variety of the fish soups which are quintessentially Mediterranean in their flavour are often made with white wine. As always there are great exceptions to the rule such as the *kakavia* of the Greek fisherman which does not include wine.

Good-quality red and white wines are also at home with rice in such dishes as seafood risotto, *arroz negro con alioli,* the Greek *mithia pilaf* (rice with mussels), or the Majorcan rice with crab and saffron. In all these recipes it is a good idea to cook with the wine you are intending to serve at the table.

Wine will always improve the most humble meat stews and casseroles. The *stifatho* of the Greeks, the *estouffade de boeuf* from the Camargue, the *stracotti* of the Tuscans and the *rabo de toro* (ox tail) from Andalusia are all stews cooked with red wine, but there are many other beef and poultry dishes in the Mediterranean in which white wine is favoured.

My recipe for poussins (squab) in a garlic, thyme, bay and wine sauce (see page 48) is a good example. Roasting meat, poultry and fish with white wine has become an essential part of my everyday cooking. For excellent results all you need is a large earthenware dish, a decent size chicken or a leg of lamb, quails or patridges, and always a little olive oil and wine. Fresh herbs and garlic can be added but this is very much a question of personal taste. Wine supplements a number of fish dishes and delicious as well as simple is the serving of any member of the sea bream family or the superb sea bass on a bed of potatoes or a selection of vegetables such as fennel, spring onions (scallions), shallots and carrots. Remember that the wine should be added only once the meat or fish has been sealed first by the heat of the oven for a few minutes.

Among the many desserts which can be prepared with wine, summer and winter fruit compotes are particularly good with dry or sweet wines. Vanilla ice cream is transformed by a hearty sauce of oloroso Sherry and the combination of spices, brown sugar, wine and fruit with peaches (see page 98) is a revelation.

POUSSINS / SQUAB IN A GARLIC, THYME, BAY AND WINE SAUCE

I am convinced that one of the secrets behind the success of this dish is the superb and very heavy frying pan/wok I use which allows the sauce to combine and reduce as it should.

SERVES 2

150 ML / 5 FL OZ / ⅔ CUP OLIVE OIL

2 POUSSINS (SQUAB), CUT IN HALF

6 GARLIC CLOVES, PEELED AND SLICED (3–4 SLICES PER CLOVE)

A PINCH OF DRIED THYME

2 BAY LEAVES

200 ML / 7 FL OZ / SCANT CUP DRY WHITE WINE

SALT AND FRESHLY GROUND PEPPER

In a deep frying pan heat the olive oil and seal the poussins on each side over a high heat for 6 to 8 minutes or until well browned and nearly cooked through. Add the garlic, thyme and bay leaves followed by the wine, and immediately cover the pan to protect yourself from a splattering as the wine comes into contact with the hot olive oil. Reduce the heat and simmer, covered, for 10 to 12 minutes or until the poussins are tender. (Adding wine to the hot oil produces an emulsion which, if overcooked, will separate, so check after approximately 7 minutes to make sure that the sauce looks creamy. If not, remove from the heat, add a little hot water and return to the heat to finish cooking.) Season. Do not overcook the sauce; when ready it should be creamy in colour and consistency.

Serve with grilled artichokes and potato purée. Caramelized yellow peppers (see page 34) are also a good complement to this very tasty dish.

Small Hake with Fresh Herbs

This is a family recipe using hake, the fish for which Spaniards are prepared to pay any price because quality and freshness are paramount to its flavour. In Castilian, finas hierbas *does not necessarily coincide with the French term* fines herbes, *it simply means fresh herbs.*

Serves 4

250 G / 8 OZ MUSHROOMS, SLICED

4 TABLESPOONS FRESH PARSLEY, FINELY CHOPPED

½ TEASPOON FRESH TARRAGON, FINELY CHOPPED

1 TABLESPOON LEMON JUICE

4 TABLESPOONS WHITE WINE

3 TABLESPOONS EXTRA-VIRGIN OLIVE OIL

4 SMALL HAKE, ABOUT 300 G / 10 OZ EACH, CLEANED AND HEADS REMOVED

SALT

Combine the mushrooms, parsley, tarragon and half of the lemon juice in a bowl and mix well. Add the wine and olive oil and mix again.

Place the mushroom mixture in an ovenproof dish and bake in the oven preheated to 180°C/350°F/gas mark 4 for 5 minutes.

Season the fish with a little salt and the rest of the lemon juice. Add the fish to the ovenproof dish, return to the oven and bake for a further 8 to 9 minutes or until the fish and mushrooms are cooked through.

MONKFISH STEW WITH WINE, PEPPERS AND ALMONDS

Suquet is the name given to the traditional Catalan fish and
shellfish stews to which different types of sauces are added at the
beginning and the end of the cooking of the dish.
This is my personal version of a suquet.

SERVES 6

1.5 KG / 3 LB MONKFISH, SKINNED AND GREY MEMBRANE REMOVED

2 RED SWEET PEPPERS

750 ML / 1¼ PINTS / 2½ CUPS / COLD WATER

200 ML / 7 FL OZ / SCANT CUP EXTRA-VIRGIN OLIVE OIL

2 CARROTS, PEELED AND FINELY CHOPPED

1 BAY LEAF

2 ONIONS, PEELED AND SLICED

6 RIPE TOMATOES, PEELED AND CHOPPED

1 WINE GLASS DRY WHITE WINE

2 TABLESPOONS FLOUR, MIXED IN A LITTLE WATER

3 GARLIC CLOVES, PEELED AND SLICED

50 G / 1½ OZ / ⅓ CUP FRESH (RAW) ALMONDS, PEELED

8–10 SAFFRON THREADS, SOAKED IN BOILED WATER FOR 20 MINUTES

200 G / 7 OZ / 1⅓ CUPS SHELLED FRESH PEAS

SALT

Remove the bone from the monkfish (reserve the bone for making the stock) and cut the flesh into 4 pieces. Set aside.

Impale the peppers on a long fork and roast over an open flame until the skin starts to darken and separate from the flesh. Keeping the pepper on the fork, hold under cool running water and remove the skin. Halve, remove the seeds and pith and then slice into thick strips. Set aside.

Put the fish bones (if available) and skin in a large saucepan and cover with the cold water. Bring slowly to the boil and simmer for 30 minutes. Strain into a clean pan and boil to reduce to 500 ml / 16 fl oz / 2 cups.

Heat half of the olive oil in an earthenware dish or *cazuela*. When hot, add the carrots, bay leaf and onions and cook until the onions are translucent and tender, taking care not to brown them. Add the tomatoes and cook until tender and broken down, then add the wine. Cook until the liquid has reduced by half. Discard the bay leaf. Stir in the flour and remove from the heat. Purée the mixture in an electric blender. Pass through a sieve to remove the tomato seeds. Return the mixture to the *cazuela*, add the fish stock and bring to the boil. Cook for a further 10 to 15 minutes.

Pound the garlic, almonds and saffron in a mortar and pestle to make a paste. Add the paste to the tomato and stock mixture, stir well and cook for a further 2 to 3 minutes.

In a separate pan, cook the peas in boiling salted water. Drain.

Season the pieces of fish with salt. Pour the rest of the oil into a baking dish or another *cazuela* and place in the oven, preheated to 180°C / 350°F / gas mark 4. When the oil is hot, add the pieces of fish. Return to the oven and bake for 4 to 5 minutes. Pour the sauce over the fish and add the peas and peppers. Bake for a further 4 to 5 minutes. Do not overcook the fish. Serve immediately.

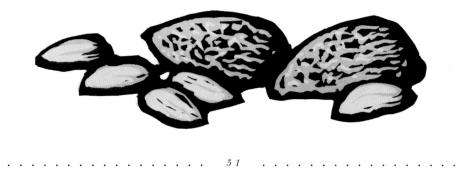

Simple Risotto with Lamb's Kidneys, Fresh Thyme and Caramelized Onions

*This dish works best in the spring when the lamb is tender
and lamb's kidneys are small and, for my taste, at their best.*

Serves 4

4 tablespoons olive oil

100 g / 3½ oz baby onions, peeled (leaving the root intact) and halved if large

1 garlic clove, peeled and finely chopped

1 tablespoon fresh thyme leaves

2 small fresh lamb's kidneys, trimmed and sliced

2 tablespoons dry white wine or lemon juice

For the risotto:

1.2 litres / 2 pints / 4 cups light poultry stock

30 g / 1 oz / 2 tablespoons butter, plus a small piece

1 small onion, peeled and finely chopped

375 g / 12 oz / 1½ cups Italian risotto (arborio) rice

4 tablespoons dry white wine

Salt and freshly ground pepper

Freshly grated Parmesan cheese (optional)

First, start the risotto. Place the stock in a saucepan over a low heat. Heat the butter and oil in a large deep frying pan. When hot, add the chopped onion and cook over a moderate heat for 3 to 5 minutes or until softened and beginning to colour.

Meanwhile, begin preparing the caramelized onions. Heat the olive oil in a small saucepan and, when hot, add the baby onions. Cover, reduce the heat and cook gently for 20 to 25 minutes or until golden and caramelized, stirring occasionally.

Continue the risotto: add the rice to the pan and stir thoroughly to coat all the grains with butter. Add the wine and stir until it has been absorbed. Begin adding the hot stock, a ladleful at a time, ensuring that each addition is absorbed before adding the next. When all the stock is used, the rice should be cooked and still firm. Remove the pan from the heat. Add the seasoning, the extra small piece of butter and Parmesan if using. Allow to sit while you finish the onions.

Remove the lid from the onions and add the garlic, thyme and kidneys. Stir once, then add the white wine or lemon juice and stir well to deglaze the pan. Continue cooking over a low heat for 3 to 5 minutes or until the kidneys are just cooked. Season, and stir this mixture into the risotto. Serve immediately.

A FRUIT COMPOTE

Use the best wine you can afford to prepare this compote.

SERVES 4 TO 6

2 COOKING APPLES

1 PEAR

1 PEACH

2 APRICOTS

200 G / 7 OZ MIXED BLACK, PURPLE AND WHITE GRAPES

1 LITRE / 1¾ PINT / 1 QUART WATER

200 G / 7 OZ / SCANT CUP SUGAR

500 ML / 16 FL OZ / 2 CUPS RED WINE

50 G / 1½ OZ / ½ CUP WILD STRAWBERRIES

Peel the apples, pear, peach, apricots and grapes, reserving all the skins. Cut all the fruit, with the exception of the grapes and strawberries, into medium-sized pieces, discarding cores and seeds.

Bring the water to the boil in a large saucepan and gently poach each fruit individually until tender, in the following order: pear, peach, apricots and lastly the apples. Do not overcook. Remove the fruit with a slotted spoon and place in a serving dish. Bring the cooking liquid to the boil once again, add the skins and cook until tender.

Strain the liquid into a small saucepan, discarding the skins. Bring to the boil and stir in half of the sugar. Reduce until a syrup is achieved. Pour it over the prepared fruit and place the fresh grapes on top.

In a small saucepan simmer the red wine with the remaining sugar for 5 to 6 minutes. Set aside to cool.

Spoon the wine syrup over the fruit and place the wild strawberries on top. Serve with rice cream (see page 106).

OX TONGUE WITH CLOVES AND WINE

The final dish will compensate for the difficulty you may encounter in preparing the ox tongue. This recipe is also excellent served cold with a salad and boiled potatoes dressed with olive oil and parsley.

SERVES 8

1.5 KG / 3 LB OX TONGUE

100 ML / 3½ FL OZ / 7 TABLESPOONS OLIVE OIL

2 CARROTS, PEELED AND CHOPPED

2 ONIONS, PEELED AND CHOPPED

1 LARGE LEEK, CHOPPED

2 STALKS CELERY, CHOPPED

3 TOMATOES, PEELED AND CHOPPED

2 WHOLE CLOVES

150 ML / 5 FL OZ / ⅔ CUP OLOROSO SHERRY

SALT

To prepare the tongue, put it in a large pan of boiling water and blanch for 10 minutes. Refresh in cold water and drain. Peel the tongue.

Heat the olive oil in a large saucepan and sauté the vegetables for 10 to 15 minutes or until tender and beginning to colour. Add the tongue and cloves and cover with water. Bring to the boil, then reduce the heat and simmer for 1 to 2 hours or until the tongue is very tender. Remove the meat and purée the vegetable sauce. Return the sauce to the pan and add the oloroso Sherry. Simmer until the Sherry has been absorbed, then season with salt.

Cut the tongue into thin slices and serve with the vegetable sauce. Mashed potatoes with a dash of nutmeg would be a good accompaniment.

SPICY HOT WINE

I don't know where this recipe comes from, but I do know that in the long winter months in our house in London it has become a warm and welcoming aperitif that tastes of the spices of the Orient, the oranges of Valencia and the wines of Sicily.

SERVES 6

1 BOTTLE OF GOOD-QUALITY RED WINE

PEEL AND SEGMENTS OF 1 ORANGE

JUICE OF 1 ORANGE

20 G / ¾ OZ / 1 TABLESPOON SUGAR OR TO TASTE

2 WHOLE CLOVES

GRATED NUTMEG TO TASTE

A GRINDING OF BLACK PEPPER

100 ML / 3½ FL OZ / 7 TABLESPOONS BRANDY

Place the wine, orange peel, segments and juice, and sugar in a large pan. Stir a little to dissolve the sugar. Add the spices and bring to the boil. Reduce the heat and simmer until a white foam appears on the surface of the wine. Add the brandy, bring back to the boil and set alight. Burn for a few seconds, then blow out the flames.

Place a few orange segments from the wine in each glass and strain the wine into the glasses. Serve very hot.

BREAD, FLAT OR FLUFFY

The beautiful medieval walled city of Morella in the Spanish Levante is most famous for its black truffle market and yet my memories of this fascinating place are of the tantalizing aroma of freshly baked bread. In Morella bread is still baked in the traditional way with a good-quality flour. Mariano Sanz is one of the three master bakers of the city. He once outlined the process of breadmaking to me: 'It's so easy,' he said. 'Take 500 grams of flour, 250 cc of water, 15 to 20 grams of fresh yeast and a little salt. Dissolve the yeast in 2 to 3 tablespoons of tepid water and set aside. Start adding water to the flour little by little, add the yeast and then begin to knead. With patience and energy your dough will become elastic and soft. Let it rise and bake it.' Well, we all know that it is a little more complicated than that but it is in everyone's power to enjoy the experience of making bread.

In the Mediterranean world bread is life: it is a treat and a necessity, it belongs to God and has been baked since time immemorial (the ancient Egyptians understood the secrets of fermentation). Today every country and every village around the sea still has access to the raw materials for baking real bread, even if the modern world threatens the continuity of traditional ways. Flat or fluffy, big or small, round or oval, elongated or short, soft or crisp, simple or embellished with seeds, nuts or fruits, with olive oil or without olive oil, it is a much loved food, particularly when hot from the oven.

The names given to the breads of the Mediterranean are richly descriptive. *Carta da musica* is a lace bread from Sardinia. The *pan de palles* rubbed with fresh tomatoes and olive oil, known as *paamb tomàquet*, is the delight of the Catalan breakfast table, while I believe that the Greeks are the master bakers of olive bread or *eliopsomo*. In Morocco, sesame seeds and aniseed are a very important feature of the tasty *kisra* or *khboz* and in Sicily religious festivals are associated with the baking in large wooden ovens of the traditional semolina breads (see page 64). There are also bread-based dishes which do not require washing up. These are called *cocas* in the Balearic Islands, *pissaladiera* in southern France, *khboz bishemar* in Morocco and *pizza* all over the world (see page 116).

Having tried and failed several times to bake a flat bread, I saw through the glass door of my oven the round and expanding silhouette of a Turkish pitta bread and realized I wanted to bring back the taste and smell of the bread baked in the wonderful lunchtime restaurants near Istanbul's spice market. My pitta breads have a lovely taste (see pages 66) even if they lack the superb flavour of the donner kebab juices poured over the pitta by a friendly chef. I have also to confess that the breads baked in southern Italy are another of my weaknesses (see page 72). I do not know if I adore them for what they are or because they remind me of the specialities of my beloved Iberian Peninsula (see page 62). Often baked in wooden ovens out-side the house, these large round breads have a hard and crisp exterior but a tender heart. The secret is the semolina flour which can now be found in many places outside Italy.

In all these recipes I have had to take into consideration the restrictions imposed by a small domestic oven and the difficulties of finding the right type of flour. I use fresh yeast, unbleached flours ground the old way, my hands for kneading, and dough starters, which make life easier while baking and produce bread which tastes like heaven. The Italians call their starters *biga* and the Spaniards *madre* or mother. They are simply doughs prepared in advance with water and flour but without salt. They will substitute or reduce some of the ingredients during the proper baking of the breads while enhancing the flavour. I would recommend the use of a baking stone in the oven which are now available on the market.

In this book I have tried to reproduce recipes which have delighted both my palate and my mind while travelling in the Mediterranean, and I have to confess that from the very beginning this chapter in particular has been both a challenge and a treat.

IBERIAN BREAD

A baking stone is what you need if you want to bake the crisp, crusted
and spongy textured breads (known as hogazas*) popular in Spain and*
Portugal. Prepare the starter dough the night before (with this quantity,
you will have enough to bake loaves for 3 consecutive days.)
To keep it in the right condition, knead the starter dough for a few
minutes every day and add a little extra flour and water.
Use your hands to prepare the starter dough.

MAKES ONE OBLONG LOAF

FOR THE STARTER DOUGH:

10 G / ⅓ OZ FRESH YEAST

250 ML / 8 FL OZ / 1 CUP TEPID WATER

500 G / 1 LB / 4 CUPS TYPE '00' FLOUR

FOR THE SECOND DOUGH:

10 G / ⅓ OZ FRESH YEAST

250 ML / 8 FL OZ / 1 CUP TEPID WATER

1 TEASPOON MALT EXTRACT

250 G / 8 OZ UNBLEACHED STRONG PLAIN FLOUR
(1⅔ CUPS UNBLEACHED ALL-PURPOSE FLOUR)

150 G / 5 OZ STONEGROUND WHOLEMEAL FLOUR
(1 CUP STONEGROUND WHOLE-WHEAT FLOUR)

8 G / ¼ OZ / ½ TABLESPOON SALT

OLIVE OIL FOR GREASING

To make the starter dough, dissolve the yeast in 2 to 3 tablespoons of the
tepid water. Place the flour in a bowl with the yeast mixture and add the
remaining water a little at a time, mixing it in very lightly with your hands.
The mixture will be rather sticky, but will improve as more water is added.

Transfer the dough to your working surface, previously sprinkled with flour, and knead for about 10 minutes or until smooth and elastic. Grease a bowl with a little olive oil, place the dough in the bowl and cover with a damp tea towel. Set aside in a cool place or the refrigerator to rise overnight.

For the second dough, place the yeast in a large mixing bowl with a couple of tablespoons of the tepid water. Stir to dissolve, then leave to rest for 5 minutes. Dissolve the malt extract in the remaining water and add it to the yeast. Add 150 g / 5 oz of the starter dough and mix well until blended. Add the flours and salt in several batches, incorporating each addition well before adding the next. Once evenly mixed, tip the dough on to a floured work surface and knead for 10 to 15 minutes or until smooth and elastic.

Place the dough in an oiled bowl, oiling the surface of the dough to prevent a skin forming. Cover and leave to rise at room temperature, or slightly cooler, for 3 hours or until the dough has doubled in bulk.

Punch the dough to knock out any air, and turn on to a lightly floured surface. Knead briefly, and form into an oblong loaf. Slash the surface 4 or 5 times with a very sharp knife. Place on a floured baking sheet or baking (pizza) peel, cover with a clean towel and leave to rise at room temperature for about 1 hour or until doubled in size.

Half an hour before baking, preheat the oven at the highest temperature with a baking stone inside. When the bread has risen, slide it on to the hot stone. Reduce the oven to 220°C / 425°F / gas mark 7 and bake for 40 to 50 minutes or until golden and well risen. The bread should sound hollow when tapped on the base. Cool on a wire rack.

SEMOLINA BREAD

I have tasted wonderful breads made with 100% semolina flour in Morocco,
and in Sicily where they are known as pane rimacinato, *but they need to be*
baked in a wood-fired oven. This bread uses a relatively small
amount of semolina and it has been baked in a rather boring domestic oven,
but the result is just as delicious. I wonder if I would be allowed to build
a clay oven in our communal garden?

MAKES 2 LARGE ROUND LOAVES

FOR THE STARTER DOUGH:

5 G / ⅙ OZ FRESH YEAST

250 ML / 8 FL OZ / 1 CUP TEPID WATER

500 G / 1 LB / 4 CUPS TYPE '00' FLOUR

OLIVE OIL FOR GREASING

FOR THE SECOND DOUGH:

15 G / ½ OZ FRESH YEAST

250 ML / 8 FL OZ / 1 CUP TEPID WATER

1 TEASPOON MALT EXTRACT

250 G / 8 OZ / 2 CUPS TYPE '00' FLOUR

150 G / 5 OZ / ¾ CUP SEMOLINA FLOUR

12 G / 2 TEASPOONS SALT

CORNMEAL FOR SPRINKLING

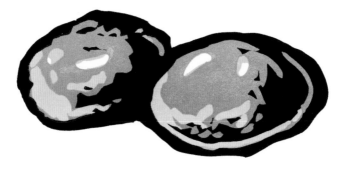

The night before you wish to bake the bread make the starter dough. Dissolve the yeast in a little of the water. Add the remaining water, then begin adding the flour and mix until all the flour has been incorporated. Mix this dough by hand. Place the dough in an oiled bowl, cover with a damp cloth and leave in a cool place or the refrigerator to rise for at least 12 hours.

For the second dough, dissolve the yeast in a little of the tepid water in a large mixing bowl. Dissolve the malt extract in the remaining water and add to the yeast. Add the starter dough and mix well until smooth. Add the flours and salt in several batches, mixing well between each addition until fully incorporated. Mix to make a fairly heavy dough that is not sticky.

Turn the dough on to a floured work surface and knead for 10 to 15 minutes or until smooth and elastic. Form the dough into a ball and place in an oiled bowl, oiling the surface of the dough to avoid a skin forming. Cover with a damp cloth and leave to rise at room temperature for 3 hours or until doubled in bulk.

Punch the dough to knock out air, and tip on to a lightly floured work surface. Knead briefly, then cut the dough in two equal pieces. Form each piece into a ball and place on floured baking sheets or baking peels. Cover with a heavy cloth and leave to rise at room temperature for 1 to 1½ hours or until doubled in size.

Half an hour before baking, preheat the oven at the highest temperature with a baking stone inside. When ready to bake, sprinkle the baking stone with cornmeal and slide the loaves on to the hot stone, leaving a few inches between them to allow for expansion. Reduce the oven to 220°C / 425°F / gas mark 7 and bake for 60 to 70 minutes or until crisp and brown. The loaves should sound hollow when tapped on the base. Cool on a wire rack.

FLAT BREADS

It was a Canadian and not an Arab who encouraged me to bake flat breads. Naomi Duguid is a distinguished photographer and the most enthusiastic flat bread maker I know. With this recipe I have tried to follow her teaching.

MAKES 10 TO 12

15 G / ½ OZ FRESH YEAST

250 ML / 8 FL OZ / 1 CUP TEPID WATER

1 TABLESPOON OLIVE OIL, PLUS EXTRA FOR GREASING

½ TEASPOON SALT

*500 G / 1 LB UNBLEACHED STRONG PLAIN FLOUR
(4 CUPS UNBLEACHED ALL-PURPOSE FLOUR)*

In a large mixing bowl, dissolve the yeast in a few spoonfuls of the tepid water. Add the rest of the water and the olive oil and stir a little with a spoon. Add the salt and then, using your hands, start mixing in the flour little by little until you have a soft dough.

Turn the dough on to a well-floured work surface and knead vigorously for about 12 minutes, adding a little more flour if necessary. By then, the dough should be smooth, elastic and no longer sticky. Shape the dough into a ball.

Coat a large mixing bowl with a little olive oil and place the ball of dough in it, turning to coat the dough with oil all over to prevent a skin from forming. Cover the bowl with a damp towel and leave to rise at room temperature for 1½ to 2 hours or until doubled in bulk.

Turn the dough on to a floured surface and punch it to knock out air. Knead briefly, then divide into 10 to 12 equally small pieces. Flour your hands and roll each piece of dough into a small ball. Leave them to rest for 5 minutes, which will make rolling out easier.

Sprinkle your work surface with more flour. Using your hands or a small rolling pin, flatten the balls into ovals that measure about 20 x 10 cm / 8 x 4 inches. Sprinkle flour on a clean cloth and place the bread ovals on top. Cover with another cloth and leave to rise at room temperature for 20 to 30 minutes or until doubled in size.

Meanwhile, preheat the oven at the highest temperature; after 15 minutes place a non-stick baking sheet inside. (It is important that the baking sheet is hot when you place the pittas on it.) Brush each pitta with a little water to avoid over-browning, then place on the hot sheets. Reduce the oven to 220°C / 425°F / gas mark 7 and bake for 6 to 8 minutes. The bread will puff up dramatically after about 2 to 3 minutes. Cool on a wire rack, then wrap in a clean towel to keep them soft.

TUNA, ONION, TOMATO AND RED PEPPER FLAT BREADS

The bread dough I have used to prepare this dish comes from the Turkish kiymali pide although I have substituted the traditional Turkish stuffing of minced meat and onion with the tuna, onion and tomato filling which is my favourite.

MAKES 8

FOR THE DOUGH:

15 G / ½ OZ FRESH YEAST

35 ML / 1¼ FL OZ / 2½ TABLESPOONS TEPID MILK

500 G / 1 LB UNBLEACHED STRONG PLAIN FLOUR
(4 CUPS UNBLEACHED ALL-PURPOSE FLOUR)

60 G / 2 OZ / 4 TABLESPOONS BUTTER, SOFTENED

2 EGGS

1 TEASPOON SALT

35 ML / 2½ TABLESPOONS TEPID WATER

1 EGG YOLK, BEATEN, TO BRUSH FLAT BREADS PRIOR TO BAKING

FOR THE FILLING:

2 SMALL ONIONS, PEELED AND VERY FINELY CHOPPED

2 SMALL RED SWEET PEPPERS, SEEDED AND CUT VERY SMALL

2 RIPE TOMATOES, PEELED, SEEDED AND CHOPPED

EXTRA-VIRGIN OLIVE OIL FOR DRESSING

A LITTLE SALT (IF NEEDED)

FRESHLY GROUND BLACK PEPPER

1 CAN (200 G / 7 OZ) GOOD-QUALITY WHITE TUNA FISH IN OLIVE OIL, DRAINED AND FLAKED

Dissolve the yeast in the tepid milk. Sift the flour in a large mixing bowl, make a well in the centre and add the yeast, butter, eggs, salt and water. Knead into a soft dough. Place in a clean bowl, cover with a cloth, and leave to rise at room temperature for about 3 hours or until doubled in bulk.

Meanwhile, mix together all the vegetables for the filling. Add 1 to 2 tablespoons of olive oil and season with salt and pepper. Mix in the tuna. Set aside.

Turn the dough on to a well-floured work surface and punch to knock out air. Knead briefly, then cut into 8 portions. With your fingers or a small, light rolling pin flatten the portions of dough into rounds or ovals. Add 1 or 2 spoonfuls of the filling to each piece of dough, ensuring that there is no excess liquid (this would seep into the dough and the flat breads would not be crisp when cooked). Roll the edge of the dough inwards to make a rim that will prevent the topping from spilling out. Set aside to rise at room temperature for 45 minutes.

Preheat the oven to 200°C / 400°F / gas mark 6, with a baking stone inside.

Brush the dough with the beaten egg yolk, then transfer the flat breads to the oven, placing them on the hot baking stone. Increase the oven temperature to 220°C / 425°F / gas mark 7 and bake for about 30 minutes.

Serve immediately.

BREAD BISCUITS

These traditional biscuits from the Majorcan town of Inca are a
wonderful alternative to bread when used in soups and even puddings.
I love them also with cheese, particularly with the Mahon cheese,
made on the island of Minorca.

MAKES 15-20

5 G / ⅙ OZ FRESH YEAST

70 ML / 2½ FL OZ / 5 TABLESPOONS TEPID MILK

35 ML / 1¼ FL OZ / 2½ TABLESPOONS TEPID WATER

70 ML / 2½ FL OZ / 5 TABLESPOONS OLIVE OIL

A LITTLE SALT

175 G / 6 OZ / 1½ CUPS TYPE '00' FLOUR

Dissolve the yeast in a little milk, then add the rest of the milk and the water. Mix in the olive oil and salt, then start adding the flour a little at a time. When all the flour has been incorporated, the dough should be very elastic, coming cleanly away from your hands.

Roll out the dough thinly on a floured surface and cut with a pastry cutter into small discs. Place on a greased baking sheet and prick each biscuit in several places with a fork. Set aside to rise at room temperature for 30 minutes.

Bake the biscuits in a preheated 200–220°C / 400–425°F / gas mark 6–7 oven for 12 to 15 minutes – they should have very little colour. Allow to cool.

FRIED BREAD IN WHITE WINE AND HONEY

There is nothing new about this recipe which is made in many countries with many variations to the list of ingredients, but this one came from the kitchen of the Cortijo de Arenales, outside the city of Seville. All over Spain during Easter the wine is substituted by milk and beaten egg and the honey by cinnamon and the resulting bread is known as torrijas.

SERVES *1*

2 SLICES OF BREAD 1–2 DAYS OLD, CUT INTO 5 CM / 2 INCH PIECES

70 ML / 2½ FL OZ / 5 TABLESPOONS WHITE WINE

1 EGG, BEATEN

OLIVE OIL FOR FRYING

1 TABLESPOON EACH HONEY AND WATER

Dip the pieces of bread in the white wine until just moist. Squeeze gently to remove any excess wine. Then dip them in the beaten egg, and fry in about 4 cm / 1½ inches of olive oil until lightly golden on both sides.

Dilute the honey with the water and drizzle over the *torrijas*. Serve hot or cold.

MODERN BREAD

This is a variation of a recipe that Pietro Peche, a distributor of quality Italian ingredients, gave me, together with the excellent flours I have been using for the past year. He calls this type of bread Pugliese. *This bread is best made in an electric mixer fitted with a dough hook, as its stickiness makes kneading difficult.*

MAKES 1 LARGE LOAF

5 G / ⅛ OZ FRESH YEAST

35 ML / 1¼ FL OZ / 2½ TABLESPOONS TEPID WATER

420 ML / 15 FL OZ / 1¾ CUPS WATER, AT ROOM TEMPERATURE

100 G / 3½ OZ STARTER DOUGH (SEE RECIPE FOR SEMOLINA BREAD, PAGE 64)

1 TABLESPOON OLIVE OIL

350 G / 12½ OZ / 3 CUPS TYPE '00' FLOUR

150 G / 5 OZ / ¾ CUP SEMOLINA FLOUR

2½ TEASPOONS SALT

CORNMEAL FOR DUSTING

Stir the yeast into the tepid water in a large mixing bowl and allow to stand for several minutes or until creamy. Add the room-temperature water, the starter dough and the olive oil and, using the paddle attachment on the mixer, mix together until smooth. Add the flours and salt and mix until the dough starts to come away from the sides of the bowl. Another 1 to 2 teaspoons of flour might be needed, though the dough should still be quite sticky at this stage. Change to the dough hook and knead at medium speed for 3 to 5 minutes or until the dough is smooth and elastic.

Tip the dough out on to a well-floured surface and, with well-floured hands, shape into a smooth ball. Place in an oiled bowl, slightly oiling the surface of the dough ball, and cover tightly with plastic film. Leave to rise at room temperature until tripled in bulk.

Punch down to knock out air, then tip out on to a well-floured surface again. Dust the dough with flour and have more flour ready for your hands. With your palms, flatten the dough gently away from you into a large oblong. Starting from the furthest short edge, roll up the dough towards you, using your thumbs as a guide to how tightly to roll it. Give the dough a quarter turn and form it into a rough ball by pulling down the sides of the dough roll and pinching them underneath with your fingertips, turning the dough as you work. Place the dough on a floured dish. Cover with a heavy cloth and leave to rise for about 1 hour or until doubled in bulk.

About half an hour before baking, preheat the oven to 220°C/425°F/gas mark 7 with a baking stone in it.

Shape the risen dough into a bolster-shaped loaf. Lightly dust it with flour and place it on a piece of non-stick baking paper. (If you sprinkle the paper with cornmeal it will give the loaf a lovely finish.) Set the loaf on the hot stone, still on the paper. Bake for 20 minutes, then remove the paper. Continue baking for 30 to 40 minutes or until golden and crusty. The loaf should sound hollow when tapped on the base. Cool on a wire rack.

AUBERGINES / EGGPLANTS AND OTHER VEGETABLES

It was only when I went to the Mediterranean markets outside Spain that I realized aubergines (eggplants) came in a number of colours: white, black, piebald and purple. The sizes and shapes were also very different from the *berenjenas* in the markets of Valencia or Barcelona. I couldn't believe how many varieties there were of this versatile vegetable (which is really a fruit). Then, when I visited Thailand, I found that this member of the *solanum* family, the *melongena*, was not a native of the Mediterranean at all: it was unknown to the Greeks and Romans and only appeared in the Mediterranean when the Arabs introduced it from India. The first written references I have found are from Islamic Spain and Sicily and were made in the thirteenth century. Nevertheless, the aubergine found the perfect habitat around the Mare Nostrum. Wherever you are – in Tunis, Poros, Aix-en-Provence or the peninsula of Daça – a delicate or spicy dish of aubergines can appear at any time. It may be prepared with cheese, or tomatoes, or puréed with lemon juice, in a roasted multi-coloured salad or in a pasta dish, the variations are numerous.

It was difficult to choose from the wealth of recipes available for inclusion in this book. In recent years an explosion of excellent writing on this ingredient has contributed to the understanding of what, only fifteen years ago, was for the tourist, the food of the locals and for the writer Elizabeth David, a romantic dream.

The aubergine is the principal ingredient of many traditional recipes such as the *moussaka* of Greece, the *ratatouille* of France and the roasted vegetable salad known as *escalivada* in Spain. A speciality from Sicily which I particularly enjoy is *caponata*, a sweet and sour aubergine sauce cooked with onions, celery, green olives, capers, tomato sauce, vinegar and sugar. And yet aubergines dusted in coarse flour and fried in hot olive oil is the way I would choose to eat them. For this simple recipe you need the large, firm and dark-coloured aubergine which my mother still buys in Spain and I buy in London's Portobello Market. Grilled with fresh mint and balsamic vinegar (see page 24), it makes a delicious dish and is equally pleasing as a cold starter. The stuffed aubergine with a chicken croquette paste (see page 78) is my personal version of a delicate béchamel dish I encountered in a village on the coastal border between Italy and France.

Sometimes I wonder how such variety and quality of fresh fruits and vegetables can be produced in the mainly dry soil and harsh weather conditions of the Mediterranean. The Romans were the first to construct irrigation systems and these were then perfected by the Arabs on otherwise unsuitable soils. The land became fertile and vegetable gardens of intense colour and tremendous variety flourished. Without aubergines, artichokes, spinach, chard, broccoli, wild mushrooms and salads of all sizes and colours, Mediterranean food would be quite different. The artichoke has now become a familiar vegetable in northern Europe but the cardoon (see page 80), a member of the same family, is harder to find outside the markets of the Mediterranean. In Spain and certain parts of southern France cardoons are synonymous with Christmas festivals, although the addition of anchovy and garlic sauce to the *cardou nissart* cooked in Nice is a foreign taste to those south of the Pyrenees.

Artichokes and cardoons are not only difficult to peel, once cleaned their colour darkens and lemon juice is often used to blanch them in cold water. If the colour concerns you then lemon is the perfect solution, but I find that the acidity of the fruit interferes with the very special flavour particular to all members of the thistle family. One thing is certain, these vegetables are an acquired taste but if you like them their preparation is a small price to pay. Borage, *borraja* in Castilian, is from the same family and is delicious cooked with potatoes and dressed with garlic and olive oil: sadly I have yet to find it outside of Spain.

If I had to choose a vegetable from the Garden of Paradise, I would choose six small artichokes and boil them in water until tender. Once drained I would heat a little extra-virgin olive oil in a saucepan and fry two unpeeled cloves of garlic together with a few pieces of cured ham. Without losing a second I would sauté the artichokes with the olive oil, garlic and ham and eat them as quickly as possible just in case someone finds me! My son, a true artichoke admirer, insists that they are equally delicious without the ham but this is a matter of taste.

Stuffed Aubergines / Eggplants
with Chicken Croquette Paste and Nutmeg

What things one can do with a robust and tasty free-range chicken!
For example, cut it in half and roast one half with white wine and olive oil,
small potatoes and dried thyme for lunch, and stuff the breast of the
other half with aubergines / eggplants, as in this recipe. You can then
prepare a delicious chicken broth with the remains.

SERVES 4 AS A FIRST COURSE

2 LARGE FRESH AUBERGINES (EGGPLANTS)

SALT AND FRESHLY GROUND PEPPER

1 CHICKEN BREAST (BREAST HALF)

1 ONION, PEELED AND HALVED

1 TOMATO, CHOPPED

A FEW BLACK PEPPERCORNS

5 TABLESPOONS EXTRA-VIRGIN OLIVE OIL, PLUS MORE FOR FRYING

5 TABLESPOONS PLAIN (ALL-PURPOSE) FLOUR

¼ TEASPOON GRATED NUTMEG

2 EGGS, SEPARATED

90–120 G / 3–4 OZ / 2–3 CUPS FRESH BREADCRUMBS

Cut the aubergines into 5 mm / ¼ inch slices, sprinkle with salt, and leave to drain for 30 minutes.

Meanwhile, place the chicken breast in a saucepan with half the onion, the tomato and a few peppercorns and cover with water. Bring slowly to the boil, then cover and simmer for 25 to 30 minutes or until the chicken breast is cooked through. Remove the chicken and set aside. Strain the stock into a clean saucepan and boil to reduce to 300 ml / 10 fl oz / 1¼ cups.

Season to taste. Remove the meat from the chicken breast and chop finely.

Chop the remaining half onion and sauté in the olive oil for about 10 minutes or until softened. Mix the flour with a little cold stock or milk until dissolved, then add to the onion and cook gently for 4 to 5 minutes or until golden. Stir in the remaining stock, bring to the boil and cook for about 20 minutes or until very thick and smooth, stirring constantly.

Add the chicken and nutmeg and stir. Remove from the heat, add the egg yolks and season generously. Set aside to cool.

Beat the egg whites lightly. Rinse the aubergine slices and pat them dry. Place a spoonful of the chicken mixture on top of one aubergine slice and cover with another. Coat the aubergine sandwich first with egg white and then with fresh breadcrumbs. Fry in plenty of olive oil until golden, and serve very hot.

CARDOON IN CHRISTMAS SAUCE

*I was very surprised to see cardoon prepared at Christmas in the South of
France, for cardoon has always been a traditional Christmas dish in Spain.
The difference is that, in France, the sauce is cooked with anchovies.*

SERVES 4

1 LARGE CARDOON

1 LEMON, HALVED

1 LITRE / 1¾ PINTS / 1 QUART WATER

25 G / ¾ OZ / 3 TABLESPOONS PLAIN (ALL-PURPOSE) FLOUR

1 TABLESPOON OLIVE OIL

JUICE OF ½ LEMON

SALT

GRATED CHEESE

GRATED HAZELNUTS

FOR THE CHRISTMAS SAUCE:

50 G / 1½ OZ / 3 TABLESPOONS BUTTER

1 TABLESPOON OLIVE OIL

3 TABLESPOONS PLAIN (ALL-PURPOSE) FLOUR

375 ML / 12 FL OZ / 1½ CUPS MILK

500 ML / 16 FL OZ / 2 CUPS VEGETABLE STOCK

GRATED NUTMEG

Remove the strings from the cardoon in the same way you would from celery. Discard the green parts and rub with lemon to prevent discoloration. Cut each stalk into 5 or 6 equal pieces.

Bring the water to the boil in a large saucepan, adding the flour, olive oil, lemon juice and some salt. Add the cardoon and simmer until tender, which will take 1 to 1½ hours depending on size. (This method of cooking keeps the cardoon white.) Once the vegetable is cooked, drain and set aside.

Prepare a béchamel using the butter, olive oil, flour and stock. Add nutmeg to taste while the sauce is cooking. The béchamel should be cooked for a minimum of 20 minutes to ensure that the flour is cooked thoroughly.

Add the pieces of cardoon to the béchamel and mix well. Place in a flameproof serving dish and sprinkle with a mixture of grated cheese and hazelnuts. Place under the grill (broiler) for a few minutes to melt the cheese and turn the topping golden in colour.

STEW OF CHICKEN, OKRA AND HERBS

I realized last Christmas that my mother had never tasted okra, for it is a vegetable you cannot find in Spain. It was in a restaurant called the Medusa in the city of Marmaris, Turkey that I first tasted a recipe very similar to this stew. Both the okra stew and the fresh apricots I had as a dessert were something to remember.

To prevent the okra losing its texture, cut the core out of the cone-shaped tops without piercing through the skin around the core. Put the okra in a bowl of water with 2 tablespoons each of vinegar and salt and leave to soak for 30 minutes.

SERVES 4

2 BREASTS (BREAST HALVES) FROM CORN-FED CHICKEN

4–5 TABLESPOONS OLIVE OIL

2 GARLIC CLOVES, PEELED AND CUT IN HALF

1 ONION, PEELED AND SLICED

300 G / 10 OZ RIPE TOMATOES, PEELED, SEEDED AND CHOPPED

250 G / 8 OZ OKRA, TRIMMED

200 G / 7 OZ COURGETTES (ZUCCHINI), SLICED

DRIED THYME TO TASTE

1 SMALL BAY LEAF

1 SMALL FRESH HOT GREEN CHILI PEPPER, SEEDED AND CHOPPED

FOR THE STOCK:

½ ONION

1 RIPE TOMATO

A FEW BLACK PEPPERCORNS

SALT

Remove the skin and bones from the chicken breasts and reserve. Cut the chicken meat into small pieces and set aside.

To prepare the stock, place the chicken bones and skin in a saucepan with the onion half, tomato and a few peppercorns. Cover with cold water and bring slowly to the boil, skimming the surface. Simmer gently for 30 minutes. Strain and reserve 300 ml / 10 fl oz / 1¼ cups of the stock.

Heat the olive oil in a large flameproof casserole, add the pieces of chicken breast and seal at a high temperature. Add the garlic just before the chicken is ready and cook briefly. Remove with a slotted spoon and set aside. Add the sliced onion to the oil and cook for 10 minutes or until softened and beginning to brown. Add the tomatoes and cook for a further 5 minutes. Return the chicken to the pot and pour in 150 ml / 5 fl oz / ⅔ cup of the chicken stock. Bring to the boil and simmer for 15 minutes. Add the rest of the vegetables, the herbs, chili pepper and remaining stock and cook until all the ingredients are tender and the flavours have blended. Season with salt before serving.

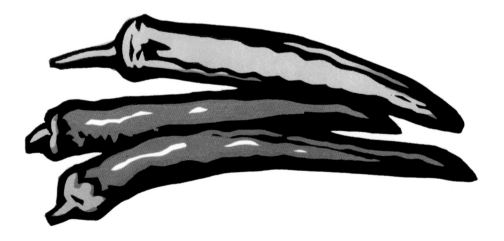

A Salad of Carrots, Pistachios, Coriander / Cilantro
and Orange Juice

Mediterranean food is travelling fast all the way to Australia. In Sydney
this particular salad and a distinguished selection of delightful meze *were*
part of the daily menu of a Cypriot restaurant in Rose Bay. As usual
the mother was the cook.

Serves 4

500 g / 1 lb carrots, peeled and thinly sliced

1 tablespoon sesame seeds, toasted

2 tablespoons fresh coriander (cilantro), chopped

1 tablespoon fresh mint, chopped

Juice of ½ orange

6 tablespoons extra-virgin olive oil

1 tablespoon ground pistachio nuts

Salt and freshly ground pepper

Blanch the carrots in boiling salted water for 2 minutes, and refresh under
cold running water. Drain thoroughly.

In a bowl combine all the ingredients. Season to taste and set aside
in the refrigerator to marinate for 2 hours. Serve with grilled aubergines
(eggplants) (see page 24).

ARTICHOKE AND FRESH PEA STEW

Winter comes and the artichoke appears in the market. In February the first early peas are tender and juicy: this is the perfect time for vegetable stews!

SERVES 4

6 SMALL TENDER GLOBE ARTICHOKES

1 LEMON, HALVED

3 TABLESPOONS OLIVE OIL

300 G / 10 OZ / 2 CUPS SHELLED FRESH PEAS

FRESHLY GROUND PEPPER

60 G / 2 OZ / ½ CUP CHEDDAR CHEESE, GRATED

150 ML / 5 FL OZ / ⅔ CUP VEGETABLE STOCK, HEATED

1–2 TABLESPOONS TOMATO PASTE

Pull any tough outer leaves from the artichokes and cut them lengthwise in half. Rub them with the lemon to avoid any discoloration. Cook the artichokes in boiling salted water for 5 to 6 minutes. Drain and set aside.

Put a little olive oil in an earthenware pot or saucepan. Add the fresh peas and arrange the artichokes on top. Sprinkle with a little pepper and some olive oil and scatter the grated cheese on top. Cook for about 5 minutes, stirring very gently to blend the cheese with the vegetables. Add the hot vegetable stock and tomato paste. Bring to the boil. Cover the pot very tightly and cook over a very low heat for about 15 minutes.

Serve with fried bread.

GRILLED SPRING ONIONS / SCALLIONS WITH A NUT AND CAYENNE PEPPER DIP

Calçots in the Catalan world of food are a type of green onion or scallion, mild and sweet, and the Calçotada is a terrific festival in which hundreds of calçots are roasted in the street and served with a Romesco sauce. Spring onions are not quite the same but they make an acceptable alternative. This dip is a perfect sauce to accompany all sorts of roasted or grilled vegetables, particularly spring onions.

SERVES 6

2 DRIED ANCHO OR POBLANO PEPPERS

1 HEAD OF GARLIC, CUT ACROSS IN HALF

1–2 RIPE TOMATOES

10 SHELLED ALMONDS, SKINNED AND LIGHTLY TOASTED

10 SHELLED HAZELNUTS, TOASTED

PINCH OF CAYENNE PEPPER OR DASH OF HOT PEPPER SAUCE

1–2 TEASPOONS RED WINE VINEGAR

2–3 TABLESPOONS EXTRA-VIRGIN OLIVE OIL

6 SPRING ONIONS (SCALLIONS) PER PERSON, TRIMMED

SALT

Roast the dried peppers in the oven preheated to 180°C/350°F/gas mark 4 for a few minutes, taking care not to burn them. Remove the stems and seeds. Place the peppers in a pan, cover with boiling water and simmer for about 20 minutes.

While the peppers are simmering, bake the garlic for 15 minutes, then add the tomatoes and bake for a further 15 minutes.

Drain the peppers. Place them in a blender, add 1 to 2 tablespoons of fresh water and purée. Peel the tomatoes and squeeze the garlic out of the skins. Add to the blender with the hazelnuts, almonds and cayenne and blend for a few minutes to make a smooth paste. With the blender still running, add the wine vinegar and season with salt. Transfer to a serving bowl and spoon the olive oil on top.

Heat a cast iron grill pan or a griddle and grill the onions with a dash of olive oil and a little coarse sea salt until they are tender and lightly charred. Serve with the dip.

POMEGRANATES, FRUITS AND NUTS

As a child, the summer meant apricots, cherries, loquats and red watermelons, then autumn came and the pomegranate ruled. This fruit divided my family: while my mother and brother found its preparation tedious and time consuming, my father and I would happily peel and de-seed all the pomegranates, then pour over a little red wine and add sugar. All this would happen an hour before lunch was served, giving the fruit time to absorb the delicious combination of wine and sugar.

The secret to pomegranates is in choosing those with skins which have begun to dry out. This indicates that the seeds are at their best, having developed the optimum balance of sweetness and acidity. You must also be certain that the fruit has not been bruised, this spoils the flesh inside.

My system for peeling pomegranates is to remove the blossom and the stem with a paring knife, then make four cuts from top to bottom taking great care not to cut deeper than the thickness of the skin. With both thumbs on the top and fingers on the bottom, break open the fruit. Patience is required when separating the pith from the sweet and juicy seeds, but it will be rewarded.

The *punica granatum*, pomegranate or *granada* in Spanish, is the symbol of fertility in Persian, Greek, Roman and Hebrew lore. It is sometimes used as an ingredient in Mediterranean cooking and at others is eaten simply as a dessert. It was in a local bar in the Andalusian city of Córdoba that I first saw the reddish crystal seeds of this fruit being used in a fresh chicory (Belgian endive) salad. There are other inventive ways of utilizing the pomegranate: I sometimes prepare grenadine, the tasty syrup which is obtained by boiling the seeds with sugar and extracting the juice. I have also made multi-coloured pomegranate sorbets and ice creams which are always popular with children. Pomegranate juice makes a delicate alternative to vinegar for dressings and marinades.

The quince is another fruit which I remember well from the two years I spent as a child in the Canary Islands. I was very small and most of the memories of that time have faded, but the days of the seashore and quinces will always remain with me. Beach vendors provided the lemon-coloured, sharp-flavoured fruit and my mother, the pesetas needed for their purchase. The trick was to take the fruit into the water and swim under the breaking waves while biting into the fruit at the same time. Quince paste or *carne de membrillo* was another delicacy, often part of the *merienda*, our daily afternoon treat, while the adults had it for breakfast cut in slices and served with fresh or matured cheese.

Moroccan and Tunisian *tagines* share the laurels in the delicious presentation of quinces. Poultry and lamb tagines are prepared with apples, pears, apricots and quinces. Suggest a fruit and a North African cook will prepare a *tagine* for you.

Classic Catalan cuisine has featured fresh fruit since medieval times in such dishes as *janet de gallina con peras y membrillos*, a hearty combination of chicken, pears, quinces, honey, almonds, bread, vinegar and seven different spices known as *salsa fina* (ginger, cinnamon, white pepper, cloves, mace, saffron and nutmeg). Dried fruit and nuts have also consistently featured in the Mediterranean cuisine bringing piquancy to the world of sauces like the Catalan *picada* or the Turkish *tarator*. Warm almond soups (see page 18) are served at Christmas in Majorca and Minorca and in the summer almond soup with garlic is chilled in Córdoba and Málaga. In Spain, almonds are ground into a paste with sugar and egg whites to create a creamy marzipan which is one of the pleasures of Christmas, and in Sicily a light green marzipan is used to decorate *cassata*, a combination of ricotta, sponge cake and candied fruit. In convents, the keepers of tradition, the nuns mould marzipan into the shape of beautiful little fruits.

I connect raisins with Moroccan food and with Andalusian Mozarabic fish and game specialities. Turkey recalls dried apricots and hazelnuts eaten in the afternoon, pistachio delight and *baklavà*. Another wonderful use of nuts is in nougat. My favourite is the dark hard almond and caramel Guirlache, followed by the soft and slightly burnt flavour of the Gijona nougat from Alicante – almost too good to eat!

SKATE WITH A CORIANDER / CILANTRO, PARSLEY AND PRESERVED LEMON SAUCE

*In Andalusia, the medieval recipe, skate with bitter orange sauce, is
prepared with garlic, parsley, bread and bitter orange peel and juice.
Preserved lemons are equally delicious when cooked with this fish.*

SERVES 4

4 PORTIONS OF VERY FRESH SKATE, EACH WEIGHING 250 G / 8 OZ

SALT AND FRESHLY GROUND PEPPER

100 G / 3½ OZ / ABOUT 3 CUPS CUBED BREAD WITHOUT CRUST

500 ML / 16 FL OZ / 2 CUPS LIGHT FISH STOCK

2 GARLIC CLOVES, PEELED AND CHOPPED

3½ TABLESPOONS FRESH PARSLEY, CHOPPED

1½ TABLESPOONS FRESH CORIANDER (CILANTRO), CHOPPED

180 ML / 6 FL OZ / ¾ CUP OLIVE OIL

2 TABLESPOONS DRY WHITE WINE

4 SMALL SLICES OF PRESERVED LEMON (SEE PAGE 94)

Season the fish with salt and set it aside for 20 minutes. Soak the bread in
200 ml / 7 fl oz of the fish stock. Drain, pressing well, and reserve the stock.
Using a pestle and mortar pound the soaked bread with the garlic, parsley
and coriander. Add half of the olive oil, a little at a time, mixing constantly
with the pestle. (You can make the paste in an electric blender if you prefer.)
Dissolve the paste in the fish stock reserved from soaking the bread. Set this
sauce aside.

Heat the rest of the olive oil in an earthenware *cazuela* or shallow
saucepan. Fry pieces of the fish for 1 minute on each side. Add the sauce
and the rest of the stock and bring to the boil. Add the wine and cook for a

few more minutes, shaking the pot constantly. Add the pieces of preserved lemon and cook for 2 to 3 minutes longer. The sauce should be reduced and all the flavours blending together. Remove the lemon pieces, and serve. If you find this recipe a little strong for your taste you can always add a little extra stock.

PRESERVED LEMONS

*I discovered preserved lemons in the Medina of Tunis. Olives and
preserved lemons are kept in large wooden drums placed outside the shops.
But this recipe was not influenced by the Tunisians:
Stephanie Alexander, the renowned Australian chef, is behind it.*

6–8 SMALL JUICY LEMONS, WELL SCRUBBED

60 G / 2 OZ / 3½ TABLESPOONS SALT

2 WHOLE CLOVES

½ CINNAMON STICK

JUICE OF 2 LARGE LEMONS

Sterilize a tall preserving jar that is just large enough to hold all the lemons
tightly packed. A 500 ml / 16 fl oz / 2 cup jug should be adequate.

Make four deep incisions in each lemon, taking care not to cut right
through. Sprinkle salt into the incisions. Pack the lemons tightly in the jar
with the cloves, cinnamon and any leftover salt. Cover with the lemon juice
and add water, if necessary, to fill the jar. Cover the jar and keep in a cool,
dry, dark place for 4 to 5 weeks before using.

Nougat Ice Cream with Sultanas / Golden Raisins and Wine

This is a rich ice cream full of Oriental flavours and nutty promises.

SERVES 6

500 ML / 16 FL OZ / 2 CUPS MILK

1 VANILLA POD (VANILLA BEAN)

6 EGG YOLKS

250 ML / 8 FL OZ / 1 CUP WHIPPING CREAM OR HEAVY CREAM

150 G / 5 OZ SPANISH GIJONA TURRON (SPANISH NOUGAT)

SMALL DECORATIVE BASKETS OF LIGHT PASTRY TO SERVE THE ICE CREAM

FOR THE SAUCE:

6 TABLESPOONS SULTANAS (GOLDEN RAISINS)

½ BOTTLE OF VERY SWEET SHERRY (PEDRO XIMENEZ)

Soak the sultanas in the Sherry for 2 days before making ice cream.

Prepare a custard for the ice cream with the milk, vanilla pod and egg yolks and chill. Whip the cream and stir into the cold custard. Blend with the *turrón* (which is very soft and slightly oily). Use an electric ice cream maker to prepare the ice cream.

Serve small portions of ice cream in pastry baskets. Pour the sultana and Sherry sauce on top at the last minute or, even better, once the ice cream baskets are already on the table.

ROAST CORN-FED CHICKEN WITH PINE NUTS AND RAISINS

Catalan food has been influenced by many different cultures but the Arabs
left behind a passion for pine nuts and raisins.

SERVES 4

A CORN-FED CHICKEN, WEIGHING ABOUT 1.5 KG / 3 LB

SALT AND FRESHLY GROUND PEPPER

1 TABLESPOON OLIVE OIL

15 G / ½ OZ / 1 TABLESPOON BUTTER

75 G / 2½ OZ / ½ CUP RAISINS, SOAKED FOR 30 MINUTES AND THEN DRAINED

75 G / 2½ OZ / ¾ CUP PINE NUTS

1 WINE GLASS OLOROSO SHERRY, WARMED

Season the chicken with salt and freshly ground pepper and brush with olive oil. Roast in the oven preheated to 200°C / 400°F / gas mark 6 for about 1½ hours or until tender and browned, basting occasionally. Transfer to a warmed serving dish.

Heat the butter and fry the raisins and pine nuts for 4 minutes. Spoon them over the chicken. Pour over the Sherry, set alight and serve while flaming.

CHICKEN OR TURKEY BREAST IN A POMEGRANATE SAUCE

*The Arabs brought to southern Spain the sophistication of Persian food
and the pomegranate. What a gift!*

SERVES 4

4 BREASTS (BREAST HALVES) FROM CORN-FED CHICKEN OR TURKEY

OLIVE OIL

1 WHITE ONION, PEELED AND FINELY CHOPPED

SEEDS AND JUICE OF 2 POMEGRANATES

120 ML / 4 FL OZ / ½ CUP DRY WHITE WINE

SALT AND FRESHLY GROUND PEPPER

In a large frying pan sauté the chicken or turkey breasts in olive oil at a high temperature until lightly browned. Remove and set aside. Add the onion to the oil and cook for about 10 minutes or until translucent, without browning. Add the pomegranate seeds and juice and the wine. Reduce the heat and simmer until the liquid thickens. Remove from the heat and blend in a food processor or blender for a few seconds. Press through a sieve and return to the pan to heat through. Return the poultry breasts to the pan and simmer in the sauce for a few more minutes or until thoroughly cooked. Season with salt and pepper, and serve.

SUMMER PEACHES WITH WINE, STAR ANISE
AND CINNAMON SYRUP

This makes a wonderful dish in the summer when you can select peaches which are firm but full of flavour. I learned from the Middle East how to combine perfectly fresh fruit, dried fruit and spices but the wine syrup originates from my mother's recipe for a winter compote.

SERVES 6

100 G / 3½ OZ / ½ CUP GRANULATED SUGAR

150 ML / 5 FL OZ / ⅔ CUP WATER

1 EGG WHITE, BEATEN UNTIL FROTHY BUT NOT STIFF

50 G / 1½ OZ / ½ CUP PINE NUTS, TOASTED

100 G / 3½ OZ / 1 CUP SHELLED PISTACHIO NUTS, ROUGHLY CHOPPED

6 MEDIUM-SIZED RIPE PEACHES, HALVED AND STONES REMOVED

JUICE OF ½ LEMON

FOR THE WINE SYRUP:

100 G / 3½ OZ / ½ CUP FIRMLY PACKED BROWN SUGAR

75 ML / 2½ FL OZ / 5 TABLESPOONS WATER

75 ML / 2½ FL OZ / 5 TABLESPOONS RED WINE

½ CINNAMON STICK

1–2 SMALL STAR ANISE

1 SMALL VANILLA POD (VANILLA BEAN)

In a small saucepan, combine the granulated sugar and water and stir gently over a low heat until all the sugar has dissolved. Raise the heat and simmer for 5 minutes to make a heavy syrup. Remove from the heat and cool slightly, then slowly pour the syrup over the beaten egg white, whisking constantly until combined.

Combine the pine nuts and pistachios in a mixing bowl. Add the egg white mixture and mix thoroughly. Set aside.

To make the wine syrup, combine the brown sugar and water in a saucepan and stir gently over a low heat until all the sugar has dissolved. Add the wine, spices and vanilla pod and simmer for 5 minutes or until you have a light syrup. Remove the vanilla pod, rinse and dry it for re-use.

Pack a large spoonful of the nut mixture in the hollow in each peach half. Arrange them in an earthenware or ovenproof dish that is just big enough to hold them in a single layer. Pour the wine syrup evenly over the peaches. Bake in the oven preheated to 190°C/375°F/gas mark 5 for 30 to 35 minutes or until tender.

Remove from the oven and allow to stand for 5 minutes before squeezing the lemon juice over the peaches, and serving.

Rice, Pasta and Couscous

Tables are set up in the sunlight and fresh bread and wild flowers are placed on the multi-coloured tablecloths. From early morning, firewood has been burning in the outdoor oven which is now ready for the first dish, a *cazuela* of rice, garlic heads and pieces of the local black pudding (blood sausage). The women are relaxing for a change: on Sundays and days of celebration in Spain the cooking of rice is done by the men.

We know that rice (the grass *oryza sativa*) was originally cultivated in North-East India and in the northern territories of Thailand. Although it had reached parts of the Mediterranean before the fifth century it was not until the eighth century that it was planted in Spain and southern Italy by the Arabs, the great agricultural innovators of the time. Today it is grown in the Camargue, the delta of the river Ebro in Catalonia, in Valencia, Andalusia, the Po Valley, Greece, Turkey and Egypt. The type of rice, method of cooking and even the utensils used are particular to different regions. Broadly speaking, in Spain and Italy short grain rice of the japonica variety is favoured; while long grain rice of the indica variety is preferred to the east of the Adriatic.

It is a feature of Mediterranean cuisine that we cannot just talk about rice, we must talk about specific rice dishes: *paella, dolma, pilaf, risotto.* Some are prepared with fish and shellfish, others with meat, game or chicken, with vegetables and even with snails. Sometimes the rice is cooked in water, sometimes in stock or wine, with olive oil or butter, with spices or without. Spain's most famous use of rice is in a *paella.* This traditional meal, devised by the farmers of Valencia, is made with chicken, rabbit, beans and spices (contrary to popular belief, the true *paella* should not contain fish or shellfish). *Paella* is also the name of the pan in which this dish is cooked. In Turkey, *pilaf* is the name given to a dish based on rice, wheat or bulgur. In Izmir *tavurku pilav* is made with chicken and rice and served at weddings. *Arroz negro* in Castilian refers to a serving of rice cooked with vegetables and the ink of squid or cuttlefish (see page 114), while *riso nero*, the Sicilian speciality, is a dessert made with milk, cocoa, cinnamon, almonds and rice. I have been told that *riso nero* is of Spanish origin, but have found nothing to back this up.

Semolina is the secret behind the breads of Sicily, Puglia and Morocco (see page 64) and what we know today as Italian pasta; it is a flour which has been ground from the hard durum wheat. But there is more to come: once it has been rolled, humidified and coated with thinner hard wheat flour, semolina becomes couscous, the staple grain of North Africa. Couscous was not a part of my food culture for *alcuzcuz*, as it was known in southern Spain during the Islamic period, has disappeared without trace from the kitchens of Andalusia. But I can remember eating couscous as a child in Ceuta and the colour of the terracotta dish in which the grains were served with a substantial vegetable, chickpea and meat stew on top. At the time, we lived in Rota near Cádiz where my father was stationed with the Spanish air force. Shopping and eating in North Africa was something my mother could not resist and family day trips across the Straits of Gibraltar were popular with us. Years later while studying in Carcassone in southern France, couscous became part of my summer diet. It was served daily in an

Algerian café, was quite delicious and was well within my modest budget.

While couscous can be served with lamb (see page 110), chicken, vegetarian or fish stews, *cuscus*, the Sicilian speciality from the city of Trapani is always served with a comforting *zuppa di pesce* (fish soup). But it was in Tunisia that I realized that what couscous is to North Africa so rice is to Valencia, Catalonia, Castellón and Alicante: a love affair with food of exquisite taste, a dish that never tires.

It appears that pasta was known to the Etruscans and the Greeks. In Spain *fideos* and small pearls of pasta known as *lluvia* were cooked well before the tenth century. These were introduced by the Arabs and are still very popular in the Catalan and Valencian cuisines. *Fideua*, cooked in the paella pan, is a fish and shellfish dish in which rice has been substituted by pasta (see page 112). In Turkey small ravioli served in a yogurt sauce is known as *manti* and in Greece *hylopittes* (small pieces of square pasta) are often served with meat and chicken dishes cooked in a tomato sauce. But if we are talking seriously about pasta we must go to Italy, where it goes far beyond the predictable spaghetti dishes which have become such a feature of modern life. In Italy pasta is an art, a symphony of shapes, textures and, above all, good taste. It is equally delicious either with a sauce, or on its own with a little olive oil and garlic. I prefer the taste and texture of dried pasta made with durum wheat but just across the road from where I live I have one of those tempting delicatessens in which two or three different types of fresh pasta can bring happiness to my table any day.

RICE WITH FRESH VEGETABLES, CHICKEN LIVERS AND HERBS

You have to be demanding about the freshness of the chicken livers for this rice dish!

SERVES 4

250 ML / 8 FL OZ / 1 CUP OLIVE OIL

2 GREEN SWEET PEPPERS, SEEDED AND CHOPPED

1 RED SWEET PEPPER, SEEDED AND CHOPPED

6 GARLIC CLOVES, PEELED AND CHOPPED

200 G / 7 OZ CHICKEN LIVERS, CHOPPED INTO LARGE PIECES

2 WHOLE CLOVES

1 BAY LEAF

1 TEASPOON DRIED THYME

6 BLACK PEPPERCORNS

400 G / 14 OZ / 2 CUPS SHORT-GRAIN RICE SUCH AS ARBORIO OR BOMBA

200 G / 7 OZ MIXED VEGETABLES, SUCH AS FRESH PEAS, FRENCH OR OTHER GREEN BEANS AND BABY LEEKS, TRIMMED AND SLICED AS NECESSARY

1.2 LITRES / 2 PINTS / 5 CUPS HOT CHICKEN STOCK (SEE PAGE 105)

Heat the oil in a shallow frying pan or earthenware *cazuela*. Add the chopped sweet peppers and garlic and sauté for about 10 minutes or until softened. Add the chicken livers, cloves, herbs and peppercorns and cook until the chicken livers are browned. Add the rice and stir well, then add the vegetables and stock and bring to the boil over a high heat. Boil for 5 minutes. Reduce the heat slightly and simmer for 5 minutes. Reduce the heat again and simmer gently for a further 10 minutes. Turn the heat down to its lowest setting and cook for 5 minutes or until the rice and vegetables are tender. The result should be a fairly liquid, soupy rice. Season to taste and serve at once.

CHICKEN STOCK

MAKES ABOUT 3 LITRES / 5 PINTS / 3 QUARTS

500 G / 1 LB CHICKEN BONES AND CARCASSES, WITH A LITTLE MEAT

3 LITRES / 5 PINTS / 3 QUARTS COLD WATER

1 TABLESPOON TOASTED AND CRUSHED SWEET DRIED PEPPERS, SUCH AS ÑORAS,
OR USE SWEET PAPRIKA

2–3 RIPE TOMATOES OR CANNED TOMATOES, HALVED

½ HEAD OF GARLIC, CUT IN HALF ACROSS AND ROASTED IN A HOT OVEN FOR 15 MINUTES
OR UNTIL SOFTENED

8–10 SAFFRON THREADS

140 ML / 4½ FL OZ / ⅔ CUP WHITE WINE

SALT

Put all the ingredients in a large cooking pot. Bring slowly to the boil, skimming off any scum that rises to the surface. Cover and simmer gently for 1 hour. Strain and discard the bones and vegetables.

RICE CREAM WITH CINNAMON AND LEMON PEEL

*Rice cream has very little to do with school dinners and many things
in common with the rice pudding desserts served all around
the Mediterranean world.*

SERVES 4

140 ML / 4½ FL OZ / ⅔ CUP SINGLE CREAM (LIGHT CREAM)

70 ML / 2½ FL OZ / 5 TABLESPOONS MILK

1½ TEASPOONS UNFLAVOURED POWDERED GELATINE

2 EGG WHITES

50 G / 1½ OZ / ¼ CUP SUGAR

GROUND CINNAMON FOR SPRINKLING

FOR THE RICE PUDDING:

500 ML / 16 FL OZ / 2 CUPS MILK

100 G / 3½ OZ / ½ CUP SHORT-GRAIN RICE SUCH AS ARBORIO OR BOMBA

50 G / 1½ OZ / ¼ CUP SUGAR

½ CINNAMON STICK

2 STRIPS OF LEMON PEEL

To make the rice pudding, place the milk, rice, sugar, cinnamon stick and lemon peel in a saucepan and bring to the boil. Simmer gently, stirring constantly, for about 20 minutes or until the rice is tender and the milk mostly absorbed. If the rice isn't ready, cook for a further 5 minutes. You may need to add a little water towards the end of the cooking time to prevent the rice from sticking. Remove from the heat and allow to cool. Remove the cinnamon stick and lemon peel.

Place half the rice pudding in a blender and process until smooth, adding a little milk if necessary. Add to the remaining rice pudding along with the cream.

Heat the milk to boiling. Remove from the heat and immediately sprinkle the gelatine over the surface. Whisk until dissolved, then stir into the rice mixture. Beat the egg whites until they will hold soft peaks. Beat in the sugar until fully incorporated. Fold a large spoonful of the egg white mixture into the rice pudding to slacken it. Add the remaining egg whites and fold in gently but thoroughly. Do not overmix.

Spoon the rice mixture into a greased mould or ramekins and refrigerate for at least 3 hours or until set.

Remove from the moulds and serve sprinkled with cinnamon or with a fresh apricot coulis.

PASTA WITH FRESH ARTICHOKES AND CURED HAM

Freshly boiled artichokes sautéed with Jamón Serrano are an important part of my culinary heritage. The addition of pasta guarantees this dish will satisfy the needs of my 22-year-old son, Daniel.

SERVES 4 TO 6

4 GLOBE ARTICHOKES

JUICE OF ½ LEMON

500 G / 1 LB SPAGHETTI

3 TABLESPOONS GOOD-QUALITY OLIVE OIL

3–4 GARLIC CLOVES, PEELED AND SLICED

150 G / 5 OZ SLICES OF HAM, SHREDDED BY HAND

SALT AND FRESHLY GROUND PEPPER

FRESHLY GRATED PARMESAN CHEESE

Bring lightly salted water to the boil in two saucepans, a very large one for the pasta and a medium-sized one for the artichokes.

Before you start preparing the artichokes, add the lemon juice to a bowl of cold water. Remove the stalk from each artichoke with a paring knife. Pull off tough outer leaves. Trim the top 2 cm / ¾ inch from each artichoke, then cut in half lengthwise and remove the hairy choke. As soon as you finish preparing an artichoke, drop it into the lemon water to stop it discolouring. When all the artichokes are prepared, drain them and drop into the boiling water. Cook for about 8 to 10 minutes or until almost tender. Drain and set aside.

Add the pasta to the large pot of boiling water. When the spaghetti is almost *al dente*, heat 3 tablespoons of olive oil in a frying pan and add the garlic. Before the garlic browns, add the pieces of ham and stir a little, then add the artichokes. Sauté all together for 1 to 2 minutes.

Drain the spaghetti and toss with the artichokes and ham. Season well with plenty of black pepper and fresh Parmesan cheese. Serve immediately.

A Classic Meat Couscous

You don't need to buy a Tunisian or Moroccan earthenware double boiler
to prepare couscous but I would recommend you treat yourself to
a good metal couscousière.

Serves 4

400 g / 14 oz boneless stewing lamb, cut into chunks

Salt and freshly ground pepper

45 g / 1½ oz / 3 tablespoons butter

2 tablespoons olive oil

1 onion, peeled and chopped

150 g / 5 oz / 1 cup potatoes, peeled and cut into chunks

120 g / 4 oz / ½ cup dried chickpeas, soaked overnight

150 g / 5 oz / 1 cup young turnips, peeled and cut in half

150 g / 5 oz / 1 cup marrow, courgettes (zucchini) or pumpkin flesh,
cut into large pieces

½ teaspoon saffron powder, or 8 saffron threads, toasted and ground

1.25 litres / 2 pints / 5 cups water

350 g / 12 oz / 2 cups couscous

150 g / 5 oz / 1 cup small carrots, peeled and each cut into 2 pieces

2 tablespoons fresh parsley, chopped

2 tablespoons fresh coriander (cilantro), chopped

A small fresh hot chili pepper

For the chili sauce:

½ teaspoon hot paprika

1 teaspoon harissa sauce (see below)

Season the lamb with salt and pepper. Heat 30 g / 1 oz / 2 tablespoons of the butter and the olive oil in the bottom of a couscousière, or whatever pan you are using to prepare the dish. When hot, add the lamb. Brown on all sides, then add the onion and cook for a further 5 minutes or until soft. Add the potatoes, chickpeas, turnips, marrow or pumpkin, and saffron and cover with the water. Bring to the boil, then cover and simmer for about 1 hour.

If you are using 'instant' couscous, follow the instructions on the packet. If you are using a more traditional couscous, moisten the grains slightly with a little cold water, stirring with your hands before tipping it into the top of the couscousière.

Add the remaining ingredients to the stew and set the top of the couscousière in place so that the couscous can steam over the simmering stew. Cook for 30 minutes. Turn the couscous into a large bowl and moisten again with a little cold water, stirring well. Return to the steamer top and cook for a further 30 minutes.

Remove the couscous to a serving dish and stir in the remaining butter until melted. Keep hot.

For the chili sauce, remove 200 ml / 7 fl oz / scant cup of the sauce from the stew and stir in the paprika, and *harissa*.

Serve the stew poured over the couscous or in a separate bowl. Pass the chili sauce separately.

Note: To make *harissa* sauce, pound 3 to 4 small dried hot red chili peppers with a peeled clove of garlic and a little salt, using a mortar and pestle. Cover the paste with olive oil and stir to mix. *Harissa* will keep for ever in a sealed jar in the refrigerator. You can use bought *harissa* sauce in this recipe if you prefer.

SEAFOOD FIDEOS

Fideua originated in the Alicantine town of Gandia in Mediterranean Spain where the rice of a traditional fish and shellfish dish was substituted for fideos – the pasta brought to Spain by the Arabs. I have given two different methods in this recipe: the traditional and the more modern way I prepare it at home.

SERVES 6

100 ML / 3½ FL OZ / 7 TABLESPOONS OLIVE OIL

300 G / 10 OZ BONELESS MONKFISH, CUT INTO CHUNKS

300 G / 10 OZ SQUID, CLEANED, BODIES CUT INTO RINGS PLUS TENTACLES

2 GARLIC CLOVES, PEELED AND CHOPPED

1 LARGE TOMATO, SKINNED AND FINELY CHOPPED

¼ TEASPOON PAPRIKA OR PIMENTON

SALT AND FRESHLY GROUND PEPPER

6 RAW PRAWNS (SHRIMP) IN SHELL (PREFERABLY DUBLIN BAY PRAWNS)

12 RAW KING PRAWNS (LARGE SHRIMP) IN SHELL

12 FRESH CLAMS IN SHELL, CLEANED

12 MUSSELS, COOKED AND REMOVED FROM SHELLS

300 G / 10 OZ SPAGHETTI

FOR THE STOCK:

OLIVE OIL

2 MEDIUM-SIZED ONIONS, PEELED AND ROUGHLY CHOPPED

6 GARLIC CLOVES, PEELED

1 LARGE TOMATO, CHOPPED

500 G / 1 LB FISH BONES

2.5 LITRES / 4 PINTS / 2½ QUARTS WATER

FOR THE PICADA:

2 GARLIC CLOVES, PEELED

3 TABLESPOONS FRESH PARSLEY, CHOPPED

For the stock, place some olive oil in a saucepan and add the chopped onions, garlic, tomato and fish bones. Pour in the water and bring to the boil. Simmer for about 15 minutes. Strain and reserve the hot stock.

The traditional method:

Heat the olive oil in a paella pan and cook the monkfish and the squid for 5 minutes. Add the chopped garlic, tomato, paprika and a little salt and cook gently for 5 more minutes. Add the prawns, clams and mussels and simmer for 3 to 4 minutes. Add the pasta, then pour in the hot fish stock. Bring to the boil and simmer for about 10 minutes.

The modern method:

Heat a little olive oil in a small saucepan, add the garlic and tomato and cook for about 5 minutes. Stir in the paprika and cook for another minute. Set aside. Put the remaining oil in a paella pan, heat and sauté the monkfish and squid for 1 minute. Add the tomato and paprika sauce and stir. Add the prawns, clams and mussels and cook for 2 minutes, then add the pasta. Pour in the hot fish stock, bring to the boil and simmer for about 10 minutes.

Meanwhile, make the *picada* by pounding together the garlic and parsley in a mortar and pestle.

Add the *picada* to the paella pan. If your oven is big enough, slide the paella pan into the oven preheated to 180°C / 350°F / gas mark 4 and cook for 5 minutes to slightly crisp the surface. If, however, your oven is not big enough, transfer the seafood mixture to a large *cazuela* to finish cooking in the oven.

BLACK RICE AND ALLIOLI SAUCE

This rice dish is adored by Italians and Spaniards but its colour is some-
times a matter of concern to my friends of other nationalities!
In the region of Valencia, black rice is cooked in a paella pan, but in certain
villages of Catalonia, I have tasted glorious versions prepared in
earthenware pots.
Sometimes squid has only a small amount of ink – not enough to obtain a
deep black sauce – which is why I recommend you buy small bags of ink
from a quality fishmonger. The allioli sauce is served
separately in a small dish.

SERVES 6

500 G / 1 LB SQUID

140 ML / 4¼ FL OZ / ⅔ CUP OLIVE OIL

2 GARLIC CLOVES, PEELED AND CHOPPED

100 G / 3½ OZ ONION, CHOPPED

225 G / 8 OZ TOMATOES, PEELED AND CHOPPED

A LITTLE PAPRIKA OR PIMENTON

400 G / 14 OZ SPANISH SHORT-GRAIN RICE (BOMBA OR CALASPARRA IF POSSIBLE)

1 LITRE / 1¾ PINTS / 1 QUART FISH STOCK OR WATER

SALT

FOR THE ALLIOLI:

3 GARLIC CLOVES, PEELED

SALT

280 ML / 9 FL OZ / 1¼ CUPS EXTRA-VIRGIN OLIVE OIL

Clean the squid: pull the head away from the body; and all the innards, including the ink sac, will come away with the head and the tentacles. Detach the ink sac by carefully pulling from the top, to avoid breaking the fragile lining of the sac. Place the ink sac in a small bowl with some water and an extra 1 or 2 small bags of ink. Once you have extracted all the coloured ink, with the help of a spoon, strain the ink and set aside. Remove the translucent 'pen' from inside the squid body. Cut the body into rings. Remove and discard the heads, and cut the tentacles into 2 or 3 pieces each.

Heat the olive oil in a paella pan that is about 40 cm / 16 inches in diameter. Add the squid followed by the garlic, onion and tomato and sauté, stirring constantly, for 2 to 3 minutes. Add the paprika or *pimentón* and the rice and stir rapidly. Next, add the stock, which must be hot, and cook at a high heat for a further 10 minutes without stirring. Add the squid ink and slightly reduce the heat. After another 10 minutes cooking, reduce the heat a little further to produce the effect of cooking on an open fire. When all the liquid has been absorbed, add salt to taste, if needed, and check the tenderness of the rice. (The grains should still be separate.) Set aside, away from the fire, to rest for a few more minutes.

To prepare the allioli, pound the garlic with a little salt into a fine paste in a pestle and mortar. (In certain parts of Mediterranean Spain, an egg yolk is added with the garlic, to help the emulsion.) Add the olive oil drop by drop, stirring constantly with the pestle. Always stir in the same direction throughout the process. The final result should be a thick, slightly white, almost translucent sauce.

A DIFFERENT PIZZA – RED MULLET, CHARD
AND SPRING ONION / SCALLION COCA

This is a Majorcan coca and the inhabitants of the Islas Afortunadas ('fortunate islands', the name given to the Balearics) would be very upset if we were to call it a pizza.

SERVES 4 TO 6

6 LARGE LEAVES OF FRESH SWISS CHARD, SHREDDED

20 SPRIGS OF PARSLEY, CHOPPED

2 GARLIC CLOVES, PEELED AND CHOPPED

3 SPRING ONIONS (SCALLIONS) CHOPPED, INCLUDING THE GREEN PARTS

3 TABLESPOONS OLIVE OIL

1 TEASPOON PAPRIKA

SALT AND FRESHLY GROUND PEPPER

6 SMALL VERY FRESH RED MULLETS, CLEANED, SCALED AND FILLETED WITH THE SKIN INTACT

FOR THE DOUGH:

1 EGG

1 TABLESPOON LARD

1 TABLESPOON OLIVE OIL

5 G / ⅙ OZ FRESH YEAST

200 ML / 7 FL OZ / SCANT CUP TEPID WATER

250 G / 8 OZ / 2 CUPS TYPE '00' FLOUR

To make the dough, in a bowl whisk the egg with the lard and olive oil until creamy. Dissolve the yeast in 2 tablespoons of the tepid water and add to the bowl. Add the flour, a little salt and the remaining water a little at a time and mix with your fingers. Transfer to a lightly floured surface and knead gently until the dough becomes pliable. Cover with a clean cloth and set aside to rise in a warm place for about 2 hours.

Roll out the dough to a round about 5 mm / ¼ inch thick and curl up the edges to make a raised border. Place on a greased baking sheet or large pizza pan.

Mix together the chard, parsley, garlic and spring onions in a bowl and dress with the olive oil, paprika, salt and pepper. Drain any excess liquid from the mixture, then spread over the dough. Place the mullet fillets on top, skin side up, so that each portion of pizza will have two fillets. Bake in the oven preheated to 190°C / 375°F / gas mark 5 for 20 minutes or until the base is crisp and brown and the fish cooked through. Serve immediately.

BEANS AND WINTER FOOD

Last year I was invited to speak at a conference in Boston on the diets of the Mediterranean. The subject was a delightful one: the food of my childhood. I decided to start in the following way. At school, Monday was lentil day. We had chickpeas on Tuesdays and broad beans (fava beans) on Wednesdays. Thursday was the day of the pinto bean and Friday, the potato. On Saturday my mother would prepare a sumptuous stew of vegetables with meat. Sunday was the day of rice.

This may appear to be a very spartan diet with Catholic overtones but the reality was that the dried beans, which on their own sound rather dull, would be combined with all sorts of things like grains, green vegetables, garlic, ham, herbs, spices and olive oil. What a delicious school lunch they made!

Lentils, chickpeas and broad beans belong to the old Mediterranean. The lentil, probably a native of India, has been cultivated along the eastern side of the Mediterranean since Neolithic times. The Hebrews and Greeks loved the brown Egyptian varieties. In the Roman Empire recipes such as lentils with leeks, coriander (cilantro) and mushrooms, served with chestnuts or artichoke hearts were popular among the wealthy while boiled versions were the staple food of the army.

The Carthaginians introduced the chickpea to the Iberian Peninsula. Today the traditional *ollas* and *cocidos*, chickpea stews made with vegetables and meat, are an important part of the Andalusian, Catalan and Castilian cuisines and in the western Mediterranean, the French, Italians and Spaniards have created superb chickpea stews to which cured hams and sausages are added. The chickpea is also the essential ingredient in the *falafel* – a hugely popular food in Syria, the Lebanon, Jordan and Israel. It was originally prepared with dried broad beans by the Egyptians – the masters of the *falafel*. This version is easy to make: white broad beans soaked in water overnight are pounded together with onion, garlic, parsley or fresh coriander (cilantro), ground coriander, cumin, cayenne pepper and a small amount of baking powder. Small, flat, rounded portions are shaped by hand and then deep-fried in vegetable oil. Chickpeas also give *hummus* its distinctive taste and this is a food which could tempt me to become vegetarian. The delicious creamy combination of chickpeas, lemon juice, garlic, cumin, olive oil and *tahini* (pounded sesame seeds) is another wonderful present brought to the Mediterranean from the Middle East.

Another of my vegetarian dreams manifests itself as a dish of tender beans (see page 122) just removed from their pods, semi-dried then cooked with tomatoes and carrots. The Spanish call them *pochas* and they are known to the French as *flageolets*. In both France and Spain tender beans are cooked with lamb or small game. These dishes are truly unique.

Many varieties of beans came from the New World in the sixteenth century and rapidly spread to the rest of the world. Borlotti, pinto, haricot, red kidney, black-eyed, navy, black kidney, cannellini, brown and butter beans (Lima beans) all originated in the Americas. In any market around the Mediterranean at least two or three types will be on sale either dried or semi-dried depending on the season.

The Lima bean, also known as *garrafón* in Mediterranean Spain, is one of the three different beans used in the *paella* of Valencia. *Pasta e fagi-oli* is an Italian speciality which, when cooked with borlotti beans, becomes one of the best bean dishes that I know. If you are travelling in Greece or Turkey, I would strongly recommend a plate or two of the bean and vegetable salads dressed with olive oil, lemon juice and parsley available everywhere. These dishes are part of the *mezze* tradition and give you a true taste of Mediterranean food.

STEW OF TENDER BEANS AND OTHER SPRING VEGETABLES

My vegetarian friends have often complained to me that many Mediterranean stews and vegetable dishes are prepared with meat or animal fat. This delicious stew will be sure to please them as it uses only olive oil. I particularly recommend this recipe to all those keen gardeners who like to grow their own beans.

SERVES 4

1.5 KG / 3 LB YOUNG BEANS, JUST SEPARATED FROM THEIR PODS

2 LITRES / 3½ PINTS / 2 QUARTS WATER

1 ONION, PEELED AND CHOPPED

2 LEEKS, CUT INTO PIECES

2 CARROTS, PEELED AND CUT INTO PIECES

2 GREEN SWEET PEPPERS, SEEDED AND CHOPPED

2 GARLIC CLOVES

2 TABLESPOONS OLIVE OIL

SALT

Wash the beans and place in an earthenware *cazuela* or large saucepan. Add the water, onion, leeks, carrots, green peppers, garlic cloves, olive oil and some salt. Cook slowly over a very low heat until the beans are meltingly tender.

Before serving, stir the contents of the pot to blend the oil with the vegetable stock.

LENTIL, HERB AND HAM STEW

Try to use Puy lentils from Velay in the Auvergne for this dish. They are a little more expensive but their taste makes it worthwhile.

SERVES 4

500 G / 1 LB / 2⅓ CUPS SMALL GREEN LENTILS

½ WHITE ONION, PEELED

4 GARLIC CLOVES, 2 UNPEELED AND 2 PEELED AND SLICED

100 G / 3½ OZ PIECE OF CHORIZO SAUSAGE

100 G / 3½ OZ SLICE OF SERRANO HAM

1 HAM BONE

1 BAY LEAF

A LITTLE DRIED THYME

SALT

2 CARROTS, PEELED AND FINELY CHOPPED

3–4 TABLESPOONS OLIVE OIL

½ TEASPOON SWEET PAPRIKA

Soak the lentils for a few hours in cold water, then drain and rinse.

Place them in a large pan or flameproof earthenware *cazuela*. Cover with fresh cold water and add the onion half, 2 unpeeled garlic cloves, the chorizo sausage, cured ham, ham bone, bay leaf, thyme and a little salt. Bring to the boil, then reduce the heat and simmer until the vegetables are almost tender. Add the carrots and continue simmering until all are tender.

Meanwhile, heat the olive oil in a frying pan, add the sliced garlic and cook for 1 minute. Remove from the heat and quickly stir in the paprika. Wait to allow the paprika to settle to the bottom of the pan then transfer the orange-coloured garlic-flavoured oil to the stew. Stir, and serve.

Chard and Basil Soupy Rice

I like this dish because I can make it even if I have a rotten day at the office.

It is popular with my family, easy to make and very comforting food.

Serves 4

300 g / 10 oz fresh Swiss chard, roughly shredded

1 litre / 1¾ pints / 1 quart water

Salt and freshly ground pepper

200 g / 7 oz / 1 cup short-grain rice such as arborio or bomba

1 garlic clove, peeled

6 –7 fresh basil leaves

3 tablespoons freshly grated Mahon or Parmesan cheese

2 tablespoons olive oil

A little fresh lemon juice to taste

Cook the chard in the lightly salted boiling water for about 5 minutes or until almost tender. Add the rice and cook for a further 15 minutes or until tender. Season to taste.

Meanwhile, with a pestle and mortar, pound the garlic, basil leaves, cheese and olive oil to a paste. Stir the basil and olive oil paste into the rice and add a little fresh lemon juice to taste. Serve immediately.

Cod and Potatoes in a Garlic, Parsley and Pine Nut Sauce

This dish is a Catalan creation: the pine nut sauce is the medieval picada – *one of the flavours that defines Catalan food – and the cod is an ingredient which appears in more than two hundred recipes from this region.*

Serves 6

750 g / 1½ lb thick salt cod fillet, soaked and cut into pieces

Flour for coating

3 tablespoons olive oil, plus more for frying

300 g / 10 oz ripe tomatoes

750 g / 1½ lb potatoes, peeled and cut into irregular chunks

400 ml / 14 fl oz / 1¾ cups fish stock

For the pine nut sauce:

75 g / 2½ oz / ½ cup toasted almonds

75g / 2½ oz / ½ cup toasted pine nuts

2 tablespoons fresh flat-leaf parsley, chopped

1 garlic clove, peeled

20 g / ⅔ oz ground digestive biscuit (¼ cup graham cracker crumbs)

For the allioli:

2–3 garlic cloves, peeled and chopped

1 teaspoon salt

100 ml / 3½ fl oz / 7 tablespoons extra-virgin olive oil

To make the pine nut sauce, pound the almonds, pine nuts, parsley, garlic and crumbs to a fine paste in a pestle and mortar. Set aside.

Coat each piece of cod with flour. Heat enough olive oil in a frying pan so the cod will just be covered and fry each piece of cod until golden and cooked, turning once. Place the fish on paper towels to drain off any excess oil.

Grate the tomatoes to make a purée; discard the skins. Heat an earthenware pot, add the 3 tablespoons of olive oil and cook the tomato purée for about 10 minutes. Add the pine nut sauce and stir, then add the potatoes and cook for a few minutes, stirring well. Add the fish stock, a ladleful at a time. Bring to the boil and simmer for a further 10 minutes.

Meanwhile, make the allioli (this recipe does not call for an emulsion of garlic and olive oil, but a light unemulsified liquid). Simply pound the garlic and salt in a mortar and pestle, then stir in the oil.

Carefully place the pieces of fish in the pot, in between the potatoes. Spoon the allioli into the stew, shake the pot until all the ingredients blend properly and serve.

Pasta and Bean Stew

This is my personal version of the Italian dish pasta e fagioli.

SERVES 4

160 G / 5½ OZ / ¾ CUP DRIED PINTO BEANS, SOAKED OVERNIGHT

2–3 TABLESPOONS OLIVE OIL

½ ONION, PEELED AND CHOPPED

2 SMALL CARROTS, PEELED AND CHOPPED

2 CELERY STALKS, CHOPPED

2–3 RIPE TOMATOES, PEELED AND CHOPPED

1 HAM BONE

A PIECE OF HAM HOCK (CURED OR HONEY ROAST)

1 BAY LEAF

A LITTLE DRIED THYME

SALT AND FRESHLY GROUND PEPPER

200 G / 7 OZ / 1 CUP MACARONI

Drain the pinto beans and rinse with fresh water. Place the beans in a large pot and cover with cold water (do not season the beans with salt as this will prevent them becoming tender). Bring to the boil and boil for a few minutes, then reduce the heat and simmer until the beans are tender.

Meanwhile, heat the olive oil in a large pot and fry the onion for about 10 minutes or until translucent. Add the carrots and celery and cook for a further 5 minutes. Add the tomatoes and cook for 10 minutes longer, stirring frequently.

Add the ham bone and hock and stir. Drain the pinto beans and add to the pot. Cook for 3 to 4 minutes. Pour in enough fresh water to cover all the ingredients and add the herbs and salt. Bring to the boil, then cover the pot and cook for a further 1½ hours or until all the flavours are well blended. Stir in the pasta and simmer until just tender. Check the seasoning and serve hot.

WALNUT CAKE

*Last year fresh walnuts were available at my local market for a few weeks in
November and I used them to make this cake. Their freshness brings a
wonderful extra dimension to the cake but you can use packaged walnuts
which have the advantage of being available all year round.*

MAKES A LOAF CAKE

100 G / 3½ OZ / 7 TABLESPOONS BUTTER

200 G / 7 OZ CASTER SUGAR OR 1 CUP GRANULATED SUGAR

4 EGGS, SEPARATED

100 G / 3½ OZ PLAIN FLOUR / ⅔ CUP ALL-PURPOSE FLOUR

1 TEASPOON BAKING POWDER

2 TABLESPOONS GRAND MARNIER

200 G / 7 OZ / 1¾ CUPS WALNUTS, SLIGHTLY CRUSHED

In a large bowl, beat the butter with the sugar until a creamy, fluffy consistency is achieved. Add the egg yolks, flour, baking powder, Grand Marnier and crushed walnuts and mix together.

In another bowl, beat the egg whites to stiff peaks. Fold into the walnut mixture.

Grease a loaf pan and pour the walnut mixture into it. Place in the oven preheated to 190°C / 375°F / gas mark 5 and bake for about 1 hour or until risen and golden brown. A skewer inserted in the centre should come out clean. Cool in the pan.

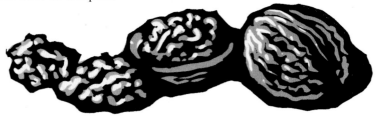

SQUID, OTHER FISH AND SHELLFISH

When I think of the Mediterranean the colours that appear before me – white, blue, green and red – are intricately linked to the sea: the white buildings contrasting with the ever-changing blue of the water, and the bright green and red fishing boats waiting in the harbour. And of course fish is central to the cuisine: the variety of both fish and shellfish available in the markets is a joy and the customer's demand for absolute freshness is something the seller expects.

The Greek writer on food and travel, Archestratus, described fish as the food of the Gods: Apollo loved turbot, Aphrodite the gilt head (a member of the bream family), Poseidon preferred the tuna fish and Zeus the sturgeon. For me, a simple mortal, sardines, anchovies, squid, red mullet and John Dory are amongst my all-time favourites.

Dried and salted fish date back to the Phoenicians who used to sail to the Straits of Gibraltar searching for trade and for tuna. Today the *salinas* or salt pans around Cádiz are a reminder of their love for salted delicacies. *Mojama* in Castilian or *missama* in Arabic are names for the dried and salted fillets of tuna, still adored by the Andalusians. *Garum*, the fermented fish sauce favoured by the Romans is definitely a thing of the past, but preserved sardines and anchovies are one of the pillars of present day Sicilian cooking. Salted and dried cod is also a treat in Catalan and Provençal specialities. The *boutargue* of the French, the *huevas* of the Spanish and the *bottargà* of the Italians is mullet or tuna roe dried, salted and pressed. In Andalusia it is thinly sliced and served as an appetizer and in Italy it is often grated over freshly cooked pasta.

The Mediterranean sardine is associated with spring and summer when it is fat and juicy. A warm summer night, fresh sardines roasted over the hot embers of a charcoal fire and a salad of locally grown tomatoes with a little olive oil: this is pure perfection to my mind. As many as four different types of this tireless traveller swim in Mediterranean waters.

Humble sardines and fresh anchovies are something that would make me travel to the Mediterranean any day. The delicious combination of pasta with wild fennel, pine kernels, sultanas (golden raisins), saffron and fresh sardines known as *pasta alla sarde* is a Sicilian speciality and a legacy of the Arabic presence on the island. The *tian* of sardines prepared around the Côte Niçoise is a layered dish with a tasty mixture of rice, spinach, Swiss chard and fresh sardines: another great combination of flavours from land and sea.

I wonder if there is anywhere in the Mediterranean which does not have a local version of fish soup or stew. The *kakavia* of the Greeks, the *bouillabaisse* of the French (see page 142) or the Ligurian *zuppa di pesce* are all variations on a theme. The *caldillo de perro* (dogs' broth) prepared around Cádiz blends the flavours of hake and the juice of bitter orange: certainly not a dish for dogs!

The family of the *cephalopods* (heads with feet) – squid, cuttlefish and octopus – belong to a world of their own and people either love or hate them. Squid, the most handsome of the three, is served deep-fried all around the Mediterranean coast. Sometimes it is stuffed with rice and fresh herbs, sometimes stewed with onions and ripe tomatoes or in a sauce of vegetables, wine and its own ink (see page 134). The secret is to know how to cook the different varieties and sizes. In my personal experience squid should either be quickly deep-fried in very hot oil or stewed until tender which can take a long time. In Mediterranean Spain, particularly in Catalonia and Valencia, *sepia* or cuttlefish is prepared *a la plancha* on a hot plate with sea salt, chopped parsley, garlic and a dash of olive oil and lemon juice. This is a wonderful dish. Delicate ragoûts made with octopus or cuttlefish are a speciality of Nice and *kalamarakia* or *soupies pilafi* (squid or cuttlefish rices) of Greece.

Large and small prawns (shrimp), clams of all sizes and textures, sea urchins and sea dates, excessively pricey and often overrated lobsters: every variety is on sale in the markets and on the marble slabs of the more specialized fishmongers. These are delicious either simply boiled, grilled on skewers and cooked *a la plancha*, or more elaborately added to dishes made with wine, pine kernels, herbs and saffron: seafood is without equal in the Mediterranean world of food.

SQUID IN ITS OWN INK, WHITE RICE AND CARAMELIZED SWEET PEPPERS

Although this recipe is not a simple one and the dark colour of the dish can seem a bit off-putting to those who have not tasted the delicious squid ink-based sauces, once tried it will become a must in any adventurous cook's repertoire.

SERVES 4

1 KG / 2 LB SQUID, CLEANED (INK RESERVED) AND BODIES CUT INTO RINGS PLUS TENTACLES

1 SMALL ONION, PEELED AND CHOPPED

200 ML / 7 FL OZ / SCANT CUP OLIVE OIL

2 GREEN SWEET PEPPERS, SEEDED AND CHOPPED

3–4 GARLIC CLOVES, PEELED AND CHOPPED

3 TOMATOES, PEELED AND CHOPPED

5 TABLESPOONS DRY WHITE WINE

SALT AND FRESHLY GROUND PEPPER

6 TABLESPOONS RED WINE

7 TABLESPOONS / ½ CUP WATER

FRESHLY COOKED WHITE RICE

Put the ink sac from the squid in a bowl and add a little water. (You may find that for a deep colour you will need 1 or 2 extra small bags of ink, available from your fishmonger.) Press to extract the colour from the ink sac, then strain the ink and set aside.

Cook the onion in half of the olive oil in a frying pan over a low heat for 10 minutes. Add the green peppers and the chopped garlic and continue cooking for 15 minutes or until all the vegetables are tender. Add the tomatoes and cook for a further 5 minutes.

Using an electric blender, mix the ink and the white wine, adding the extra bags of ink at this point if needed. Transfer the cooked tomato sauce to the blender and purée with the ink mixture, then rub the resulting sauce through a fine metal sieve.

Heat the remaining olive oil in an earthenware *cazuela*. When hot, add the squid. Season with salt. Cover the pan and cook for 2 to 3 minutes or until lightly golden. Add the tomato sauce and stir well. Add the red wine and water to the squid and bring to the boil. Reduce the heat and simmer very gently for about 1 hour.

Serve with boiled rice, caramelized peppers (page 34) and small triangles of fried bread.

FRIED OYSTERS IN CORNMEAL

*Maize and chilies came from the Americas in the sixteenth century,
moving East at a great speed. This is an alternative to fresh oysters
served with Tabasco sauce.*

SERVES 4

8 FRESH OYSTERS

JUICE OF 1 LEMON

2 EGGS, BEATEN

CORNMEAL, FOR COATING

OLIVE OIL FOR FRYING

HOT CHILI SAUCE (OPTIONAL)

Ask your fishmonger to open the oysters for you.

With a knife, remove the oysters from their shells. Sprinkle them
with a little lemon juice then dip them in beaten egg and coat with cornmeal. Fry them in very hot olive oil until golden. Place each oyster back in
its bottom shell and serve with chili sauce.

GRILLED SCALLOPS / SEA SCALLOPS ON THEIR SHELLS

If you like delicious scallops prepared in a matter of minutes,
try this recipe.

SERVES 4

8 FRESH SCALLOPS IN SHELL (SEA SCALLOPS)

4 TABLESPOONS OLIVE OIL

75 G / 3 OZ / ⅓ CUP FINELY CHOPPED ONION

2 TEASPOONS FRESH PARSLEY, CHOPPED

DRY WHITE WINE

SALT AND FRESHLY GROUND PEPPER

Open the scallops with a sturdy knife. Scrape off the beard-like fringe from around the white scallop meat, and remove the black intestinal thread. Slide a sharp knife under the scallops and remove both the scallop and the coral from the shell. Scrub the shells thoroughly.

Place a scallop in each rounded bottom shell. Add a little olive oil, onion, parsley, wine, salt and pepper. Place them under the grill (broiler) for 1 or 2 minutes. Do not overcook. Serve at once.

RED MULLET WITH ANCHOVY PASTE AND BLACK OLIVES

The Provençals love freshly caught rouget (red mullet), anchovies and – above all – black olives. They also produce sweet olive oils which I have used to fry this fish.

SERVES 6

6 SMALL RED MULLETS, CLEANED, WITH HEADS INTACT

SALT AND FRESHLY GROUND PEPPER

1 TEASPOON FENNEL SEEDS, LIGHTLY CRUSHED

JUICE OF 1 LEMON

4–5 TABLESPOONS EXTRA-VIRGIN OLIVE OIL

6 GOOD-QUALITY CANNED ANCHOVIES, DRAINED

2 GARLIC CLOVES, PEELED AND FINELY CHOPPED

2 SHALLOTS, PEELED AND FINELY CHOPPED

125 G / 4 OZ / ½ CUP BLACK OLIVES, PITTED

1 ONION, PEELED AND FINELY CHOPPED

OLIVE OIL FOR FRYING

500 G / 1 LB RIPE TOMATOES, SKINNED, SEEDED AND CHOPPED

3 TABLESPOONS FLOUR, FOR COATING FISH

6 SLICES OF BREAD, ABOUT THE SAME SIZE AS THE FISH

1 TABLESPOON FRESH PARSLEY, CHOPPED

Arrange the fish in a shallow dish and season with salt, pepper and the crushed fennel seeds. Add half of the lemon juice and drizzle with a little virgin olive oil. Leave the fish to marinate for about an hour.

Pound the anchovies with 1 garlic clove, 1 shallot, 2 tablespoons virgin olive oil and half of the olives in a pestle and mortar to make a smooth paste. Or, if you prefer, use an electric blender.

Heat a little olive oil in a frying pan and sauté the onion and remaining shallot. Add the second garlic clove and cook until slightly golden in colour, then add the tomatoes and season with salt and pepper. Cook for 15 minutes on a very low heat.

Press the tomato sauce through a sieve and return to the pan. Add the rest of the olives. Bring back to the boil, then reduce the heat and simmer for a few more minutes or until hot.

Meanwhile, heat plenty of olive oil in a large frying pan. Dip the fish in the flour and fry them at a high temperature until golden brown on both sides and just cooked.

Toast the bread and, while hot, spread with a thin layer of the anchovy paste. Place a fried fish on top of each toast. Add the rest of the anchovy paste to the tomato sauce and pour over the fish. Sprinkle the parsley on top and serve immediately.

BAKED SEA BREAM WITH MARINATED COURGETTES / ZUCCHINI

*Sea bream baked in the oven with wine and lemon is one of my
family Christmas specialities. Last year I broke with tradition
by offering this dish instead.*

SERVES 4

150 G / 5 OZ SMALL COURGETTES (ZUCCHINI), THINLY SLICED

OLIVE OIL, FOR FRYING AND MARINADE

JUICE OF ½ LEMON

SALT AND FRESHLY GROUND PEPPER

*1 SEA BREAM (PORGY) FILLETED INTO 4 PORTIONS BY YOUR FISHMONGER (KEEP THE BONES
FOR THE SAUCE)*

FOR THE SAUCE:

1 SHALLOT, PEELED AND CHOPPED

OLIVE OIL

100 G / 3½ OZ FISH BONES (FROM THE SEA BREAM)

100 ML / 3½ FL OZ / 7 TABLESPOONS RED VERMOUTH

100 ML / 3½ FL OZ / 7 TABLESPOONS WATER

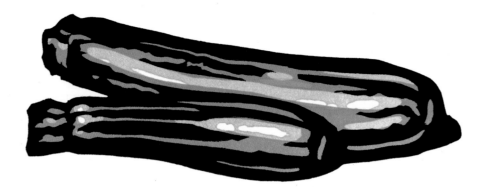

Sauté the courgettes in a little olive oil; drain on paper towels and allow to cool. In a large bowl prepare a marinade with the lemon juice, 5 or 6 tablespoons olive oil, salt and pepper. Marinate the courgettes for 20 minutes.

For the sauce, soften the shallot in a little olive oil. Add the fish bones and stir for a minute or so, then add the vermouth and set it alight. Add the water and bring to the boil. Strain into a clean pan, discarding the vegetables and fish bones. Bring back to the boil and reduce by half. Season and keep warm on a very low heat.

Season the fish fillets with salt. Heat a film of olive oil in a frying pan and lightly brown the fillets on both sides. Transfer the fillets to a baking dish, skin side up, and place in the oven preheated to 200°C / 400°F / gas mark 6. Cook for 1 to 2 minutes. Remove the dish from the oven and spoon the marinated courgettes on top of the fish. Return to the oven and cook for another minute. Serve with the sauce and stewed fennel, if you like.

SCALLOP / SEA SCALLOP, SPRING VEGETABLE AND CORIANDER / CILANTRO SOUP

It takes a long time to prepare this orange-coloured, complex fish and vegetable soup with French overtones. It is served on New Year's Eve at home – for adults only.

SERVES 4 AS A FIRST COURSE (OR 2 HUNGRY PEOPLE)

1 CARROT, PEELED AND SLICED

1 COURGETTE (ZUCCHINI), SLICED

¼ SMALL FENNEL BULB, SLICED

A FEW FRENCH OR OTHER GREEN BEANS

2 TABLESPOONS SHELLED FRESH PEAS

1 SAVOY CABBAGE LEAF, SHREDDED

4 SMALL LEEKS, WHITE PARTS ONLY, SLICED

2 TABLESPOONS CANNED HARICOT (NAVY), CANNELLINI OR BUTTER BEANS

2 TOMATOES, PEELED AND CHOPPED

SALT AND FRESHLY GROUND PEPPER

4 SHELLED FRESH SCALLOPS (SEA SCALLOPS)

A FEW FRESH CORIANDER LEAVES (CILANTRO), TO GARNISH

FOR THE SHELLFISH BROTH:

½ ONION, PEELED AND FINELY CHOPPED

1 TABLESPOON OLIVE OIL

16 FRESH MUSSELS, WELL SCRUBBED

1 SPRIG OF FRESH THYME

4–5 BLACK PEPPERCORNS

400 ML / 14 FL OZ / 1¾ CUPS FRESH WATER

FOR THE CORIANDER AND GARLIC BUTTER:

130 G / 4¼ OZ / 8 TABLESPOONS BUTTER, SOFTENED

3 TABLESPOONS FRESH CORIANDER (CILANTRO), FINELY CHOPPED

1 GARLIC CLOVE, PEELED AND CRUSHED

1 TEASPOON EXTRA-VIRGIN OLIVE OIL

Using the same pan of boiling water, blanch the vegetables for 1 to 2 minutes in the following order: carrot, courgette, fennel, green beans, fresh peas, the Savoy cabbage and leeks. As each is blanched refresh in iced water. Reserve 300 ml / 10 fl oz / 1¼ cups of the blanching liquid.

For the shellfish broth, soften the onion in the olive oil in a large saucepan. Add the mussels, thyme and peppercorns and cover with the cold water. Bring to the boil and simmer until all the mussels are open. Remove the mussels from the liquid and set aside.

Add the liquid reserved from the blanched vegetables to the broth and bring to the boil. Add the blanched vegetables, canned beans and tomatoes and cook until slightly tender. Blend until smooth. Return to the pan and season. Keep hot.

Mash together the ingredients for the coriander and garlic butter. Season to taste.

Place the scallops in a flameproof dish and dot with some of the coriander and garlic butter. Cook under a preheated grill (broiler) for about 4 minutes or until just opaque and heated through. Do not overcook. Add the rest of the coriander and garlic butter to the vegetable soup.

Pour a little soup into each soup plate, add 1 scallop and 4 mussels in the centre, and garnish with coriander leaves.

FRIED FISH WITH GREEN SWEET PEPPER SAUCE
AND CHILI SAUCE

*Clara Maria de Amezua, the Spanish food writer, is behind the
combination of the flavours in these two sauces.*

SERVES 4

2.5 LITRES / 4¼ PINTS / 2½ QUARTS LAGER / BEER

125 G / 4 OZ PLAIN FLOUR (1 CUP ALL-PURPOSE FLOUR)

SALT AND FRESHLY GROUND PEPPER

OLIVE OIL FOR FRYING

350 G / 12 OZ BONELESS MONKFISH, CUT INTO 4 CM / 1½ INCH PIECES

500 G / 1 LB RAW PRAWNS (SHRIMP, PEELED) (PREFERABLY DUBLIN BAY PRAWNS)

500 G / 1 LB SQUID, CLEANED AND BODIES CUT INTO RINGS, PLUS TENTACLES

FOR THE GREEN PEPPER SAUCE:

1 GREEN SWEET PEPPER

100 ML / 3½ FL OZ / 7 TABLESPOONS OLIVE OIL

1 GARLIC CLOVE, PEELED AND CHOPPED

2–3 TABLESPOONS WINE VINEGAR

1 TABLESPOON FRESH CORIANDER (CILANTRO), CHOPPED

FOR THE CHILI SAUCE:

1 FRESH HOT CHILI PEPPER

3 DRIED ANCHO PEPPERS

2 GARLIC CLOVES

200 ML / 7 FL OZ / SCANT CUP OLIVE OIL

1 TEASPOON GROUND CUMIN

2–3 TABLESPOONS WINE VINEGAR

To prepare the green pepper sauce, hold the green pepper over a flame until the skin is blackened all over (or char under the grill [broiler] if you prefer). Peel under cool running water. Chop the flesh and purée in a blender with all the other sauce ingredients. Season.

To prepare the chili sauce, place the fresh chili pepper and the dried *ancho* pepper in water and bring to the boil. Cook for 10 to 15 minutes then drain. Remove the seeds and cut the peppers into pieces. Blend until smooth with the remaining sauce ingredients. Season with salt. Set the two sauces aside.

Mix together the beer, flour and a little salt until smooth. Leave to rest for about 1 hour.

Heat about 4 cm / 1½ inches of olive oil in a large frying pan. When hot, dip the monkfish in the beer batter and add to the pan. Fry until golden, then remove with a slotted spoon and drain on paper towels. Keep hot while you coat and fry the Dublin Bay prawns and squid.

Serve all the fish hot, with the sauces.

LAMB, POULTRY AND SMALL GAME

Throughout history, meat has been a significant food of the Mediterranean. Its use has differed according to the various cultures and regions. For example, pork meat and products are forbidden by the Moslem and Jewish faiths, but it plays a large part in the cuisine of the Christians in France, Spain, Italy and Greece. I for one cannot imagine a lentil stew without the sumptuous flavours of a ham bone. A wonderful example of this is found in Castelnaudary, France where *cassoulet* is a mixture of beans cooked with fresh pork, sausages and crackling.

Climatic and geographical conditions affect the raising of cattle and this has led to beef being restricted to certain areas. In southern France, northern Italy and northern Spain there's a good selection of recipes prepared with beef, while in drier regions with poorer grasslands such dishes are rare. Poultry, once the food of the rich and the Christmas treat of the poor, is now widely available and yet this results in meat which is often bland and flavourless. However, there is hope: delicious free-range and corn-fed fowl are also available although at a higher price. Perhaps the best solution is for meat to be served as a treat once a week and in small helpings. Traditionally, this is the Mediterranean way of eating meat.

Lamb is loved by all. Young lamb is preferred by some while mutton is considered the best in many areas, particularly in North Africa and the Levant. In Italy and Spain, the arrival of the spring and Easter are celebrated with the new season's lamb. The Romans of today prepare young lamb by pan-roasting it with wine vinegar, anchovy fillets, rosemary and sage.

In the Emilia-Romagna region, lamb from slightly larger animals is also pan-roasted but this time with wine. In Spain the *cordero pascual* (Easter lamb) is roasted in wood-fired ovens with vinegar. Wine and different types of *aderezos* – the name given to a combination of ingredients such as onions, fresh herbs, paprika and wine – are also a traditional way of preparing larger cuts of lamb.

Roasted lamb served in a large earthenware dish (see page 150) reminds me of Tunisia and convivial lunches under a large Berber tent. In Djerba, *tagines* of lamb or chicken are made with quinces, and in every city and town the vegetable and lamb stews come with couscous and *harissa* sauce (see page 111). My memories of Greece and Turkey are of cooking in the open air using skewers of meat and vegetables, the aroma of herbs sprinkled on the fire to flavour the food, the arrival of the hot bread at the table.

The cooking of small game is also popular around the Mediterranean and game dishes are varied and original. The Moroccan pigeon (squab) or chicken pie *bisteeya* is prepared with the thinnest of pastries, almonds and cinammon. Poussin (squab) in a sauce of garlic, thyme and wine (see page 48) is what I cook when I need a superb dish in a hurry.

I first tasted *tavuk gogsu* in Istanbul. This creamy combination of rice, water, chicken, milk and sugar makes a great dessert which surprisingly does not taste of chicken. It reminds me of the medieval Catalan main course *menjar blanco de gallina* cooked with a boiling-hen, onions, almonds, rice flour, rose water and sugar. Even if the medieval version lives on only in the memory of food historians, similar dishes are prepared today in France, Spain and Sicily. French *blancmange* (sweet and bitter almonds, water, gelatine and sugar), Catalan *menjar blanco* (almonds, rice flour, cornflour [cornstarch], sugar, grated lemon rind and vanilla) and the Sicilian *biancomangiare* cooked with milk, lemon peel, candied squash and sugar are all presents brought by Arabs from the East.

Salted and wind-dried legs of pork from the European and Iberian breeds, Jamón Serrano and Jamón Ibérico are festive food for the Spaniards. Gone are the days of the *Matanza*: the celebration of the killing of the pig in November, a family ritual that preceeded the annual production of hot and sweet cured sausages, substantial black and white puddings (blood sausage), *butifarras* and hams. Yet, today these products are still made by firms following the same traditions. The exquisite cured hams from Parma, the *chorizo* my father used to buy in an old Castilian village, the superb *cotechino* that Mauro Bregolli makes in England using pork meat, spices and red wine, all belong to the same culture that uses common sense and good taste when preserving the foods once needed for survival.

But finally, fresh chicken livers pan-fried with caramelized onions (see page 152), a dash of Sherry, chopped parsley and coriander (cilantro); chicken with preserved lemons and olives; fried sweetbreads with nothing but a piece of bread to clean up the pan . . . How could I live without meat?

SUNDAY ROAST

For me, the pan juices from this roast are the best!

SERVES 4

1.2 KG / 2½ LB LEG OF SPRING LAMB

OLIVE OIL

12 SMALL POTATOES OR NEW POTATOES, UNPEELED

4 SMALL ONIONS, UNPEELED, WITH A CROSS CUT ON TOP

2 DIFFERENT COLOURED SWEET PEPPERS, QUARTERED AND SEEDED

1 HEAD OF GARLIC, BROKEN INTO CLOVES, PEELED

3 SPRIGS OF FRESH THYME

2 SPRIGS OF FRESH ROSEMARY

175 ML / 6 FL OZ / ¾ CUP GOOD-QUALITY WHITE WINE

SALT AND FRESHLY GROUND PEPPER

Set the lamb in a very large earthenware pot or a roasting pan and pour a little olive oil on top. Roast in the oven preheated to 200°C / 400°F / gas mark 6 for 10 to 15 minutes, then reduce the heat slightly. While the meat is roasting, boil the potatoes, then drain.

Place all the vegetables and herbs around the meat and roast for a further 20 minutes or so. Then add the wine and continue roasting until the lamb is ready, about another ½ hour for rare meat.

Remove the lamb and set aside to rest. Pour about three-quarters of the juices from the pan and reserve. Place the pan, with the vegetables, in the oven and cook until they are golden and tender. Transfer the vegetables to a serving dish. Return the reserved juices to the pan and deglaze the bottom of the pan, stirring well. If you like you can add a little cornflour (cornstarch) to thicken the gravy. Season and serve.

MARINATED LAMB CHOPS WITH PRESERVED LEMON AND MINT

Prepare this recipe at the beginning of the summer.
The flavours are from North Africa and they remind me of the
tantalizing, rich scents of the street food there.

SERVES 4

1 TEASPOON CHOPPED PRESERVED LEMON (SEE PAGE 94)

3 TABLESPOONS JUICE FROM PRESERVED LEMONS

6 TABLESPOONS OLIVE OIL

1 GARLIC CLOVE, PEELED AND CHOPPED

1 TEASPOON FRESH MINT, FINELY CHOPPED

FRESHLY GROUND BLACK PEPPER

8 SMALL TENDER LAMB CHOPS

Mix together the preserved lemon, preserved lemon juice, olive oil, garlic, mint and pepper. Pour over the lamb and leave to marinate for about 3 hours.

Grill over hot coals, turning the chops and brushing with the marinade. Serve very hot.

CHICKEN LIVERS WITH CARAMELIZED ONIONS, SWEET PEPPERS AND WHITE RICE

The idea for this recipe, which I often prepare at home, came from one of the small tapas dishes of Spain called higaditos encebollados *which tends to be served slightly overcooked and without boiled rice. The secret is to be patient with the onions which need time to become sweet and golden.*

SERVES 2

3–4 TABLESPOONS OLIVE OIL

2 ONIONS, PEELED AND FINELY SLICED

2 GARLIC CLOVES, PEELED AND SLICED

2 TABLESPOONS WATER

500 G / 1 LB FRESH CHICKEN LIVERS, SLICED

SALT AND FRESHLY GROUND PEPPER

FRESHLY COOKED WHITE RICE

2 CARAMELIZED YELLOW PEPPERS (SEE PAGE 34), CUT INTO 4–5 SLICES

CHOPPED PARSLEY, TO GARNISH

Heat the olive oil in a deep frying pan or wok and fry the onions and garlic over a moderate heat until they turn light brown. Add the water and cook until the onions become caramelized. Increase the heat, add the chicken livers and sauté for 2 minutes. Do not overcook as the livers should be served slightly pink. Season to taste.

Serve on a bed of rice with the caramelized yellow peppers, sprinkled with fresh parsley.

Stuffed Sweet Peppers with Quails

A different approach to this recipe is slowly to roast the peppers on a griddle, turning them constantly until the skin becomes black and easy to remove. The final taste is delicious but they are difficult to handle.

Serves 4

4 red sweet peppers

A little goose fat (optional)

4 fresh quails, preferably wild, cleaned and tied

4 rashers of smoked streaky bacon (4 thick-cut slices of bacon)

1½ tablespoons olive oil

Salt and freshly ground pepper

4 tablespoons dry white wine or fino Sherry

Cut the tops off the peppers and remove seeds. Put a little goose fat into each pepper. Wrap each quail with a rasher of bacon and put into the peppers. Place the peppers in an oiled baking dish and turn them so that they are coated with oil. Season with salt and pepper. Cover with foil, place in the oven preheated to 180°C/350°F/gas mark 4 and bake for 20 minutes.

Add the wine or Sherry and bake the peppers for another 20 minutes. Then remove the foil, increase the heat and bake until the peppers are slightly brown in colour.

Remove from the oven and, while hot, skin the peppers with your fingers. Place the peppers on a serving dish. Boil to reduce the sauce and deglaze the baking dish with a little water. Serve the stuffed peppers with a drizzling of sauce.

PARTRIDGE, BEAN AND BAY STEW

Meat and bean stews are one of the flagships of the frontier food around the Pyrenees; the cassoulet of France and the pochas con codornices of Spain. In Greece, harino me fasolia is another version on the same theme. I had all these recipes in mind when I started cooking this stew.

SERVES 4

300 G / 10 OZ DRIED WHITE HARICOT BEANS / 1½ CUPS DRIED NAVY BEANS, SOAKED OVERNIGHT

1 PARTRIDGE

2 BAY LEAVES

5 TABLESPOONS OLIVE OIL

1 ONION, PEELED AND FINELY CHOPPED

5 GARLIC CLOVES, PEELED AND SLICED

¼ TEASPOON SWEET PIMENTON OR PAPRIKA

2 TOMATOES, PEELED AND CHOPPED

SALT

Drain the beans and place in a pot with the partridge and bay leaves. Cover with plenty of water – about 1.8 litres / 3 pints / 7½ cups. Bring to the boil. Simmer for 1½ to 2 hours or until the partridge and beans are tender. Remove the partridge and separate the meat from the bones. Return the meat to the bean stew.

Heat the olive oil in a frying pan and sauté the onion and garlic cloves until they start to turn golden. Add the sweet *pimentón* or paprika and the tomatoes and cook for another 2 to 3 minutes, taking care not to burn the paprika (it tends to burn very easily.)

Add the sauce to the bean stew, season and cook for a further 20 minutes. The final dish should be soupy.

A Substantial Chicken Broth with Pasta Shells

*Is this an Italian recipe or did it come from the Christians in the
Al-Andalus? Probably both. Pasta and meat dishes appear in
twelfth-century books about the food of Andalusia and North Africa, and
they are in every Italian cookery book I know.*

SERVES 4

½ BOILING CHICKEN (STEWING HEN)

½ CORN-FED CHICKEN

2–3 VEAL MARROW BONES

1 HAM BONE

2–3 CARROTS, PEELED

2 LEEKS

2 SMALL TURNIPS, PEELED

1 CELERY STALK

2.75 LITRES / 4½ PINTS / 2¾ QUARTS WATER

150 G / 5 OZ LARGE PASTA SHELLS

PARMESAN CHEESE

CHOPPED PARSLEY

Put all the ingredients, except the pasta, cheese and parsley, in a large
stock pot. Bring to the boil, skimming well, then leave to simmer gently for
2 hours, skimming occasionally as necessary. Strain the broth into a clean
pot. You should have about 2 litres / 3½ pints / 2 quarts. Boil to reduce to
1.75 litres / 3 pints / 7½ cups. Season, remembering that the cheese will add
some saltiness.

Add the pasta. Boil for a further 10 minutes or until the pasta is *al dente*.
Serve with thin slivers of Parmesan and sprinkled with parsley.

DUCK WITH DRIED FIGS

This is rich and powerful food which I have prepared following a recipe from the talented Angel Garcia, the man behind the successful Albero y Grana restaurant in London.

SERVES 4 TO 5

A FRESH WILD DUCK, WEIGHING 2–3 KG / 4½–7 LB

1½ TABLESPOONS OLIVE OIL

125 G / 4 OZ / ¾ CUP VERY FINELY CHOPPED ONION

125 G / 4 OZ / 1 CUP VERY FINELY CHOPPED CARROTS

30 G / 1 OZ PARSLEY STEMS

PINCH OF DRIED THYME

A LITTLE BAY LEAF

2 LITRES / 3½ PINTS / 2 QUARTS WHITE VEAL STOCK MIXED WITH A LITTLE TOMATO SAUCE

1 BOTTLE OF FINE PORT WINE

500 G / 1 LB DRIED FIGS

SALT AND FRESHLY GROUND PEPPER

Cut the legs and two breasts from the duck (these are the parts of the duck with most meat). Cut them into approximately 16 small pieces, with the bone – 4 pieces to each leg and breast. Set aside.

Heat the olive oil and sauté the broken-up duck carcass with the onion, carrots and herbs. Add the white veal stock and boil to reduce the liquid by half. Strain this stock and set aside.

Sauté the pieces of duck in a large frying pan until golden brown on both sides, then turn each piece skin side down in the pan, reduce the heat and cook for a further 5 minutes, so that the duck loses extra fat. (Reserve this fat to sauté vegetables.)

Transfer the pieces of duck to a saucepan and heat. Add the Port and cook until the wine is reduced by half. Add the duck stock and dried figs, bring to the boil and simmer until you have a very tasty and substantial sauce. This will take at least 30 minutes. Taste for seasoning. Set aside to cool and then remove any excess fat. Reheat for serving.

INDEX